$ 13.95

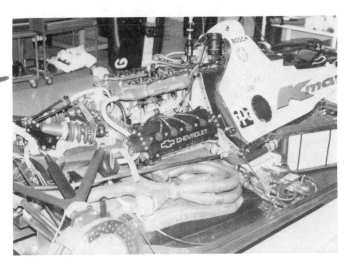

Table of Contents

Library of Congress catalog card number: 90-80544

ISBN # 09622382-3-6

Printed in the United States of America

Additional copies can be ordered from:

P.O. Box 1017 Clovis, CA 93612

Cover design by Rick Amabile and Aram Jizmejian

Rick Mears photo by Brian Spurlock

Michael Andretti photo by Dan R. Boyd

The Battle of Britain

"Why is everything built in England?" I have been asked this question countless times by curious Indy car fans. I usually go on to explain why, usually having to rely on what I've been told by various British mechanics and maybe in an occasional tiny interview with a team owner or a manufacturer. Often the trouble in explaining this was the fact that England is half way around the World so it's hard to imagine the situation if you have never been there to see the situation first hand. Before this piece, I really don't think that this subject was covered like it should be. Sure, there was a rare story in a magazine or a newspaper, but those kind of publications have limited space, therefore they usually cut a story far too short with only a few photos, if any.

A lot of people probably consider buying race cars built in England to be giving the Indy car series a black eye of sorts, but after reading this piece, I think most people will understand that that's really not the case. Certainly a country like the United States, who have been dominating the outside world when it comes to the building of aircraft and space technology, is capable of building a relatively simple race car. After all, it was always done this way from the beginning of time (1911 as far as race fans are really concerned) up until the 1980's. Certainly more recently with the TrueSports 'All American car', which sounds great in the press until you consider that it

has a British engine (sorry Chevrolet) and its designer is a Kiwi. The real question is can it be done conveniently? The answer is: not really. Convenience is a key word to the

Although only about the size of California, England is the birth place of the Worlds motor racing activity.

American public and certainly to an Indy car team owner. Do we want to buy American? Most people say "Yes, of course," but they don't usually admit they will only if it's convenient. Sometimes product A, made in America loses out to product B because, although it is made in a foreign country, product B costs less. Product A was great, but product B was selected because it was convenient to spend less. This

leads us to the racing world and creates a certain dilemma. It could be called a problem but there's really no problem. If an Indy car team elects to go out on a limb and decides to build its own car, and decides on product A, there's always the risk of failure. The easy way to go is to simply buy product B. Although not made in America, it's not only just as good, it's been proven that it's better. The main consideration in all of this thinking is of course the almighty dollar. If something works (goes fast and wins races) and is relatively cheap, you go with it. I will admit that I've created a bit of confusion when I use the word cheap in a book about Indy car racing. Certainly at about $385,000 a shot, a Lola is not cheap. But that's life in Indy car racing and if an owner chooses to bitch about this fact, he probably shouldn't be in this business to begin with. By nature race cars are suppose to be expensive. Any car that is 'cheap to build' probably shouldn't be raced. But in this instance the word 'cheap' is defined as paying $385,000 per car plus spares to the alternative. The word alternative is a scary word to the average owner. This is the practice of throwing the dice and choosing to build one's own chassis. It all sounds great in the media until you realize that the ante in this game is at least 1 million dollars to try and build one's own car. Add to this the condition that after spending huge amounts of money and time, the car can turn out to be a failure.

 **ILMOR** ENGINEERING LIMITED

HEAD OFFICE · QUARRY ROAD · BRIXWORTH · NORTHAMPTONSHIRE · NN6 9UB · ENGLAND · TEL: 0604 880 100 · FAX: 0604 882 056 · TELEX: 317406 ILMOR

In the 1960's and 70's, the motor racing industry began taking off in England. By the 1980', the country had established itself as being far ahead in the business. By this time the motor racing industry was beginning to boom, and a few astute British businessmen had already laid the foundations that would eventually make them wealthy.

The current era of the British invasion started when the now infamous Whittington Brothers purchased a pair of 'customer' cars from March Engineering. The cars were very fast straight out of the box, perhaps due to the fact that a certain amount of Formula 1 technology went into their design. Realizing that there was money to be made in the land of the free and home of the brave, there was a fight brewing in England to try to gain as big a piece of the Indy car pie as possible. The made in the U.K. lable was spawning a technological war, in our case the Battle of Britain.

I'm aboard Delta flight #1522 which is about to touch down at London's Gatwick airport. The plane decends through the clouds that never seem to end, it's another foggy day in London. I board a commuter train, headed for central London. As I look out the window, what I see really depresses me. It's cold, foggy and what we're traveling through isn't exactly one of the more modern sections of London. " Some people a long time ago sure picked a hell of a place to build a country", I thought to myself.

I'm sitting in the back seat of a taxi traveling through downtown Northampton. I get a hotel near the Cosworth factory, because I'm told that the Ilmor factory is "just down the road" from Cosworth. The prob -

lem was that I was told this information by people who live in the United States. "Just down the road" turns out to be about eight miles. " I need to find the Ilmor factory in Brixworth", I tell the taxi driver."It's in the Brixworth Industrial Estate", I say. What I later realized was that people in England, especially cab

and whip out my list of questions. "I take it that this is a big part of your life" Paul asks "Yeah, it's the only thing that I write", I reply.

In it's eight years of existence, Ilmor engineering is riding high in the saddle among engine manufacurers. Indeed, both of the

Located only three hundred yards from Paul Morgan's home, the Ilmor factory is about eight miles north of Cosworth Engineering.

drivers, have no clue that the motor racing industry exists around them. I spot the Brixworth Industrial Estate sign of the highway. "That's it", I tell the driver, but we're not out of the woods yet. After being lost for a couple of minutes, I finally see the circular Ilmor sign in the distance. I walk into the Ilmor lobby which is very quiet. I announce myself, and a moment later Paul Morgan enters and escorts me down the hall to his office. When most people do press photos, they usually clean their office for the occasion to make it look like nobody really works there. I find out that Morgan's office is always that clean. I give Paul a copy of *Inside Indy Car Racing - Volume2* ,

companie's founders, Paul Morgan and Mario Illian took upon a huge load upon their shoulders when they formed Ilmor in 1984. The financial leverage that they needed to get their dream of the ground and into the dyno room, came in the form of support from two big names in American racing: Roger Penske and General Motors. The latter wanting to break into the sport to do some heavy-duty marketing.

In the early days, the Chevy wasn't an immediate success. But, there was always the decision to stick by the engine, knowing that once the bugs were worked out, it would be a winner. It can be safely said that all of the bugs were finally worked

4

out of the engine on an April afternoon in Long Beach in 1987. Mario Andretti Scored victory number one for Chevrolet. As the count now stands as of the beginning of the 1992 season Chevy engines had scored 66 wins and are no doubt heading for the triple digits.

IICR: First of all, how long did it take to develop the first Ilmor Chevy from start to finished product ?

Paul Morgan: In the late part of 1983, Mario (Illian) and I decided that it would be a challenge to see if we could build an Indy car engine, so we got in touch with Roger Penske during November of "83 and asked him whether he would be interested in helping support the venture. He said that he'd be very interested, and wanted to know how long it would take to make the first engine and how much it would cost. We quickly got that information together and we started the company on January 1, 1984. Mario started on January 3, 1984 to design the engine on a clean sheet of paper. In the meantime, I went around and bought the field that the factory now sits on and got the plans drawn for the factory. I got the factory and the machinery on its way. Mario had finished the scheme for the engine by about March of '84, so we then hired two detail designers that could take his schemes and turn them into detail drawings for the major

castings like the cylinder block and head. The program gradually gathered pace. We had castings arrive in August to September '84 and began machining them while the

builders were still building the factory. We got some of the plant installed and finished machining the castings. The first engine sat on the dyno in the middle of May, 1985. So

Doug Wendt Photo

By having their dreams come true, Paul Morgam, 43 and Mario Illian (R), 42 have well established Chevrolet in the record books.

it took about 17 months from start to finish.

IICR: Why did you decide to build the factory in Brixworth?

Morgan: Well, principally because I lived in the village. The industrial estate on which the factory now stands was a lot smaller in those days and was just being brought up to speed. Therefore, there was the ability to buy a two acre field that we're now located on for a reasonable price. When we built the factory, it was originally 6,500 square feet. We knew that someday we would expand.

Originally the most advanced engine of its time, the Chevy A engine is now in its gray hair stages after five years of dominance.

Millions of dollars worth of high tech machines fill the main building. Many of these machines operate 16 hours a day to keep production on schedule. Pistons are being machined at the bottom of the photo.

That is in fact what happened. We designed the pipe work in a way that it would be easy and less costly to expand later in time. The factory is now at 21,000 square feet and we anticipate expanding it at some point in the future.

IICR: Did you have investors to help you buy land and build the factory before you signed the contract with General Motors ?

Morgan: Yes we did. That was Roger Penske's contribution to the Project. When Mario and I went and saw him originally, his contribution was that he was going to guarantee the finances on the engine to get it onto the dyno. Also he agreed to contact large corporations in the States who might be interested in being associated with the engine.

IICR: How many people does Ilmor employ ?

Morgan: Currently we have 116.

IICR: What was your previous background before starting Ilmor ?

Morgan: I was always interested in motor racing and I went straight from Aston University in Birmingham to work for Cosworth Engineering. I became involved in Cosworth's Indy program in 1977. I was the engineer in charge of the program from 1977 to 1984. Mario went from college at Biel in Switzerland to work for Mowag designing diesel engines before joining Cosworth in 1979. We both studied mechanical engineering. We had done one or two projects in our spare time together. We saw a unique opportunity in Indy car racing at the time. There was an engine (the Cosworth DFX) which was more or less used in every car, we felt we could make an engine that was more powerful. Also we thought the chances of a major U.S. company wanting to have a presence in Indy Car racing was high, therefore the chances of being able to get some financial backing for the project looked promising. In the racing world those two things don't often come together at once, so we thought that it was a golden opportunity which we shouldn't miss.

IICR: How many engineers do you have ?

Morgan: In broad terms, about 10.

IICR: How about assemblers?

Morgan: The actual engine shop complete is 33 people. About 17 of those are involved in the preparation of pieces of major castings from the machine shop, preparing those pieces to be assembled by an engine builder. Half of our engine shop is involved in preparing pieces and the other half is involved in assembling them. Of course we do make a lot of pieces which are exported to VDS Racing and Penske which are the two companies over in the States that rebuild our engines. They have exclusive contracts with Ilmor We have about 23 machinists.

IICR: With Mario being the engineering brains, how much does he get involved as a partner in the administration and business end of things ?

Morgan: We do tend to share the responsibilities quite widely. Mario and I spend a lot of time together discussing all of the major issues in the company. Therefore, we both know all the details of what's going on in each other's main area of activity. Most of the decisions are taken jointly.

IICR: I know why most of the cars are built in England with wind tunnels and the composite industry being so common. Is there any reason Ilmor couldn't function in America? Is it just because you lived here in the first place ?

Morgan: I think the major reason is historical. One of the other things is that European countries, not necessarily England, but European countries are different from the States because the geographical distances in the States are fairly large. The suppliers for the majority of our pieces are within an hour's drive of our factory. In the States, to be able to do the same thing, you'd probably have to jump on an airplane to go and see most of your suppliers. So that's quite a useful thing both from a speed of turn around of the actual component in

The design office. What Ilmor's competitors would give for a thorough look around !

a technical point of view, if Mario or any of the other engineers wants to go and have a look at a particular component as it's being manufacured, then the distances involved are fairly short.

IICR: Is labor a big savings in the U.K. vs. America? Is it cheaper to hire people over here than it is in the States?

Morgan: Yes, I would say that it is. It's probably cheaper to hire people here than it is in some other countries in Europe as well.

IICR: How do you bring in new people such as engineers? How much money do they make?

Morgan: It's diffucult to generalize because there are people with specialized skills who are rather expensive. We tend to bring engineers in straight from college and train them in special areas. Most of our engineers have been trained that way. It takes them a little while to become accustomed to the racing world. But when they do, we find that they're very good compared with people from outside world that have different ways of doing things.

IICR: How many resumes do you get per month from people such as college students who want to work

that we visit our suppliers on a very regular basis. Therefore, as soon as a component is ready it's continuously being worked on. From

Hundreds of design hours are saved using the famous CAD/CAM machines. Here a crankshaft part is being reviewed.

for you?

Morgan: About 3 per day.

IICR: What about assemblers and machinists? Is there ever any trouble finding people who are really good?

Morgan: I would say that finding good quality machinists is never an easy job. But I'd say that because we are a high profile company, and because we have a reputation in the locality for looking after our employees as well as we can, I think that people want to come and work for us probably more than they want to go to work for more normal industry. Therefore we tend to be fortunate in not having difficulty finding the people we need.

IICR: Would you say that the average pay for assemblers and machinists is about 15 to 20,000 pounds per year?

Morgan: That's about right, yes.

IICR: When the first Ilmor Chevy was shipped to America and was tested by Penske Racing, it had a few problems at first. Can you tell us about the problem area of the first models?

Morgan: We shipped the first engine to Penske during the fall of 1985. The major problem was with the drive between the crankshaft and the camshaft. We recognized that this was likely to be a problem on a V-8. Mario gave the situation a lot of consideration and that's one of the reasons why the camshaft gears are at the back of the engine rather than at the front. We felt that that would give the cam gears an easier time. Nevertheless, having taken as much care as we could to give the timing gears the best chance of survival, they nervertheless gave us the problem. It took us a little while to overcome the problem because it's quite a difficult one to understand. Once, we understood it, and decided what course of action to take, the pieces that needed to be made were quite a long delivery so that took a little while. But once we applied them to the engine, it was like switching on a light switch. It was the difference between night

and day instantly as far as engine reliability is concerned.

IICR: Is that the most problem part of the engine to design going in to the project?

Morgan: Yes. I think that is the area that gave us the most problems. There were obviously problems besides that, but that was the most continuous problem that we had. As far as the power of the engine was concerned, that was right from day one. I think that was one of the things that enabled the people intimately involved with the project to maintain faith in it. The first time that Rick Mears tested the engine, he knew that if it could be made reliable, it would be a winning engine. I think that was one of the major things that kept everybody enthusiastic about the project when we went through the fairly dark times of the

The Mori Seiki machine is responsible for machining the heads and blocks.

initial running on the engine.

IICR: I know that you are always trying to get the edge on the competion, but is there ever any sandbag ing that you do, like before the Cosworth came out, where you just laid back because you didn't have any serious competition? Did you decide to come out with the new

Ilmor because you are finally getting some serious competition from the people down the road?

Morgan: Well, I don't think that you can say that we actually sandbagged. What we do is to try and run a commercial business. The Indy world has always been one that is very keenly aware of the cost of going racing. I would say that the Indy teams are a very good example of how to run teams on an economical basis. With all of the costs being carefully considered and not going wild with how much is being spent. Therefore, we have had a few instances of developing components where the performance benefit is not outstanding. In other words, it's a small gain, but it's not an outstanding one. We discuss the cost with the customers and they feel that they would prefer not to use it because they don't think that it's good value for money as far as improvement of performance compared to the cost of the item. The cost is always uppermost in our mind when we're doing development of this nature. Therefore, if you are in a situation where we were for the last couple of years of winning all of the races, then we think that it's not helping the customers if you spend a fortune on development and therefore, the engine becomes very expensive purely for the sake of it. That really was the logic behind what we did. We did sufficient development to be able to be sure that we knew which direction to go when the competion arrived, as it surely would. We think, therefore, that we've applied that to the best advantage in the circumstances we've now got where I'm sure that Cosworth will make a serious bid to be able to have a good engine.

IICR: The new Ilmor B model, is it a totally new engine?

Morgan: Yes, from the crank centerline upwards, it's a completely new engine. There aren't any common pieces with the old engine.

IICR: When did you start on the new engine?

IICR: Over the last two of three years, a lot of the mid to smaller budget teams were complaining that it was unfair that they couldn't get a chevy engine. In 1991, some smaller teams were given Chevy contracts. I'm sure that these teams went to their sponsors asking for more money, telling them that all they needed to win was a Chevy engine. But then some teams were granted Chevys like Bettenhausen Motorsports and Dick Simon Racing really didn't do anything. Is it tough to go to these smaller teams and say hey, you guys just don't have it ? Whether it be the driver, the team or the equipment. It's already been proven that you can get the best engine, but without all of the other elements, it's not going to work.

Morgan: Well, I think that it's very important to remember that most big teams started off as small teams. So we always treat small teams as

potential for becoming winners in the coming years. Therefore, we always treat them seriously. One

Chevrolet B engine. Note it's slimmer and cleaner looking appearance.

of the difficulties that we've faced, in the early days, we just simply didn't have the capacity within the company to be able to make enough engines to be able to service the market. What we really

Chevrolet A engine, the powerplant that started it all.

didn't want to do was to, because it takes a long time to build a reputation, and you can lose it overnight, so what we wanted to do was to be sure that as we expanded the program, we did it in a manner in which we were sure that we could maintain engine re

liability and performance. Therefore we didn't want to get involved with smaller teams with very few engines and therefore run the engines for a long period of time and possibly have the engines fail through overuse and things like that. What we did was to supply the larger teams first of all and as soon as our capacity was able to cope with the smaller teams, then that's what we did as well. I think that we're in a better position now to be able to respond than we have been in the past. A lot of our effort over the last few years has been aimed at productivity within our company as well as improving the engine. Therefore, we should be in a position where we can supply more teams quicker in the future than we possibly have in the past.

IICR: In 1991, I believe that you began lifting restrictions by letting the individual teams play with their own fuel management systems. Is this true?

Morgan: Well, not really. Certainly we gave the teams a little more access in to the fuel management, but we've been very, very careful to retain control of the map upon which the engine runs. It's not because we think that the teams are incompetent, but the trouble is the natural enthusiasm at the race track. When you're forced in to a tight corner on fuel consumption, quite often teams are forced in to making judgements which perhaps in calmer moments you wouldn't make. Therefore, we felt that the reliability of the engine would suffer if all the teams started changing the fuel map. The one thing that we did allow the teams to do was to set the maximum speed that the engine would run. The teams have fairly good feedback on that, because if they overrev the engine too often, it costs a lot of money. We felt that was something that was perhaps a little bit appropriate to allow into the teams control.

IICR: At Indianapolis in '91, some teams were blowing Chevys at a rapid pace. I thing Galles-Kraco blew about 7 or 8 total. Is that because they were doing something wrong ?

Morgan: Not necessarily, no. We also had some other issues. One of the problems particularly at the high speed ovals such as Indy, is that you can run with the pop-off valve partially open. Sometimes you've got an unlimited supply of air, but of course you've only got a limited supply of fuel. Since the mixture of air and fuel going out of the valve is the same mixture as it would be going in to the engine, you're losing a lot of fuel and therefore the engine starts running lean. Then, piston temperature goes up very rapidly. One of the problems with the properties of aluminum is that the sort of temperatures that the piston is running at, you've only got to raise the temperature of the aluminum a small amount before you get into trouble. Therefore, the strength of the pistons is very, very dependent on their temperature. If you start running lean mixtures, you reduce the strength of the piston enormously and it will fail as a result. That is one of the common problems at Indy.

IICR: Do any of the teams tend to over engineer themselves and dial themselves out as far as fuel consumption?

Morgan: No, I don't think so. I think that most teams have got some fairly sophisticated fuel consumption programs so that they can monitor the fuel consumption in the race very well. One of the very difficult things to do is to establish what fuel consumption you've got before the race. Most teams go to the race with good intentions, but the pressures of trying to qualify well generally get in the way and that tends to be one of the lower priorities. Therefore, a lot of teams start races with not a really good feeling as to what their fuel consumption is. So over time, they've created pretty good programs to establish what it is quickly as the race progresses. Of course, the fuel meter that we have in the car is a big help.

IICR: After you draw the blueprints up for the engine, does it go straight

The dyno room. This is the birth place of all new engines.

to the machine shop?

Morgan: In the way that one would design any assembly, we start with the components that are going to take us the longest to make. That is the cylinder block and the cylinder heads. We have to go and get the patterns made for the castings. Then when the castings arrive at the factory, we start machining them. We don't actually have anything to do with the actual manufacture of the patterns or the castings. We, of course, carefully watch over them and make sure they represent what we've drawn, but we don't actually cast the blocks or the cylinder heads

ourselves.

IICR: Are the patterns wood or clay or what? Who does your casting?

Morgan: They're made in an epoxy resin. Our castings are done by Zuess Aluminum Products, they do quite a lot of castings for the motor racing world.

IICR: How many hours does it take to build and assemble an engine?

Morgan: We generally estimate that it takes about 130 to 145 hours to assemble an engine for the first time. Then about 120 hours to rebuild it, when it's rebuilt by Penske or VDS. Of course, it's not one person doing the whole thing. We don't rebuild the Indy engines here, but we rebuild the Formula One engines here. The way that we rebuild the engines, when an engine comes in, is we have a team of people that take it apart and carefully assess what needs replacing. The heads go to the head department, the pumps go to the pump department, then the rest of the engine goes to the two man team that is actually going to finally assemble the complete engine. The sub assemblers come in and the whole thing meets back and it's then bolted back together fairly swiftly. In those circumstances, you can generally turn an engine around in just over a week.

IICR: How many engines per season do the F-1 teams keep rotating?

Morgan: It's very similar to the Indy teams in fact. We feel that a single car team in the Indy car series, it's pretty uncomfortable if you have less than seven engines for one car, or fourteen engines for two cars. That's very similar to F-1 in that both the teams we support at the moment will have 15 engines a piece.

IICR: After you finally get a new engine assembled, do you just fill it up with oil, put it on the dyno and just fire it up slowly?

Morgan: Yeah, so far on all the engines that we've made, we put in on the dyno and we fire it up and run it a bit, then we stop and have a glass of Champagne! Then the fol-

Here, assemblers are rebuilding a couple of Ilmor's Formula 1 engines.

lowing day we give it a fairly hard time. We don't keep it on full throttle for long periods of time, typically an hour or something like that, on and off establishing different perameters of the engine. Then we strip it. On the second engine, providing there's nothing that looks too dire on the first, we go and start giving it the sort of treatment that it would expect to receive on the track.

IICR: Have you ever blown one up on the dyno during the first test?

Morgan: No, not the first time. They've all run pretty smoothly.

IICR: When you build an engine for the superspeedways like Indy, how many miles does it take before the engine starts to lose its power?

Morgan: Well oddly enough, it's not the power side of it that you have to be concerned about, it's whether the internal components of the engine will survive. Clearly, when you have something like a piston fail, it's a catastrophic failure. That puts the

price of the rebuild up by more than double, so it's very important that you avoid having that happen. As far as power is concerned, we often find that engines that have run 500 miles give more power after that than they have when they initially run on the dyno. It's purely because the piston rings have bedded in properly and seal the fuel better and so forth and everything's run together nicely. It's not a major amount, it's seldom more than one percent. We do find that they don't lose power in general, they tend to creep up in power. I'm using one percent as a ball park figure, but you can see an improvement in power as the engine gets older in general.

IICR: Is 500 miles the absolute limit the engine can take?

Morgan: We reckon the engine life should be reasonably safe at 500 miles. Some teams run them to 600 miles, it depends what your doing. If your doing a lot of testing and the driver is not pounding the engine hard, then you can run a few more miles. It's the pistons in general which you have to bear in mind when you put an engine through the paces.

IICR: What's harder on an engine, ovals or

road courses as far as the structure and the wear in general?

Morgan: Both have their difficulties. For instance, an oval like at Indy, the change in engine RPMs these days is very, very small. It's only about 400 RPMs between the fastest engine speed down the straight, to the slowest through the corners. It's also full throttle the majority of the time unless the driver gets in to traffic. Therefore, three hours of that sort of treatment is fairly hard on the engine. But at Indy the engine is run in a very laboratory type way, because the driver isn't changing gears very often and therefore the engine isn't being subjected to being overreved. At a road course, the driver is continuously changing gears. Sometimes in the heat of the moment, unfortunately, the driver will select the wrong gear and so the engine gets overreved. The valve gears under those circumstances get a very hard time, depending on how hard they're overreved. For instance, one of our Formula One engines got overreved to 19,000 RPMs last year, and still continued running after, which rather surprised everybody! So that's the sort of level of abuse that an engine can take at a road course. Although the race is not as long, and it's not as much full throttle, the engine has a hard time at road races as well as some place like Indy. So they're both pretty hard on an engine.

IICR: How can you overrev an engine up to 19,000 RPMs?

Morgan: Well, it just went from fifth

GM's Delco division is responsible for the Chevy's electronics package. This unit is located in the car's right sidepod.

gear to first in one shot. We were rather surprised that the wheels didn't spin, but because the engine has such a low enertia, the wheels continued gripping. It was quite interesting because with data loggers these days, you can look at it very carefully. Anyway, the driver, I don't want to mention his name, had another go at letting the clutch in at about 16,000, then finally got it down to somewhere reasonable and off he went.

IICR: What's the highest RPM that a driver has overreved an Indy engine?

Morgan: I'm not really sure. Occasionally we see them at up around 15,000 or 16,000 RPMs, which is not really good for the engine.

IICR: As far as rigidity in the block, is there any differences between ovals with their high G forces and road courses with the sudden acceleration and braking forces?

Morgan: Oh, yes. The block has obviously been designed strong enough to take the forces, but there's no doubt that places like Michigan do give the engine a fairly hard time. When we build an engine, we do actually torsionally test it on the dyno to simulate the conditions that it will see in a car, just to measure the deflections of the various major pieces. It's surprising when you actually see it happening, what a large load a racing car does put into an engine when it's just under normal cornering forces.

IICR: How much oil will a Chevy burn or lose during a 500 mile race?

Morgan: Very little actually. I can't tell you an exact figure, but it's about a couple of quarts. Not very much at all. Road courses are shorter, therefore it's even less.

IICR: Chassis manufacturers spend a lot of time in wind tunnels. Is all of your development time strictly spent on the dyno?

Morgan: No, not really. There are dynomometers of various sorts. There's development going on in all sorts of areas. We have electric motors that run some of our rigs to try to make them more economical

The all Penke front row of 1988 was made possible in great part by Chevy power. Right to left, Rick Mears, Danny Sullivan and Al Unser,Sr. Three and a half hours later, Mears would win his third Indy 500 in only 11 starts.

Political controversy was rampant until Ilmor and Chevrolet began making the A engine more available. In 1990, A.J. Foyt got his wish in the form of a Chevy lease program.

to run. We also do a huge amount of computer simulation of various things which tell us in which direction to go. The dyno is our major tool when the engine is assembled to find out how much power it gives. One of the essential things about motor racing with the fixed engine capacity formula, is that you've got to try to make the engine run as fast as you can to burn the maximum amount of air and fuel per minute to give the maximum power. Therefore there's always research into how much faster you can make the the engine go. That is quite often done with electric motors, rather that actually on the dyno.

IICR: Do you ever seek any patents on your engine pieces?

Morgan: We do ocasionally, but we don't do it much. The level of effort involved in doing it is high and by the time the patent has been granted; A)

12

you've got to disclose pretty much exactly what it is and B) you're probably on to the next development anyway. We do it, but not very much.

IICR: A few years ago, when almost every team was running Cosworths, some teams used to experiment with their own piston designs. Do any of the teams design anything like that anymore?

Morgan: No, all of the development is retained within the factory. Both Penske and VDS Racing give us continuous feedback as to how the engines look after running and send us pieces back. They keep us informed about the engine in its running state. We are fairly careful to retain the development here, although we ask them to run development bits quite often to establish whether or not they are going to be successful at the track.

IICR: What kind of fuel mileage could you get out of a Chevy if you were to convert it over to gasoline?

Morgan: It would be about twice as good. In broad terms, if you have a gallon can of methanol, it contains half the energy to a gallon can of gasoline. You have to put roughly twice the volume in to get the same amount of power.

IICR: As Indy car racing gets faster and faster on ovals, do you research different ways to limit power rather than simply cut boost pressure?

Morgan: Well, you can limit displacement obviously. I have to say that the engine power situation comes up fairly frequently in discussions, mostly involved with safety. The thing to bear in mind is that racing has to try to produce a spectacle for the fans. Because Indy cars are fairly heavy compared to other top forms of motor racing, like Formula One. I think that if the amount of power is significantly reduced, the acceleration of the car would start being unspectacular at road courses. I think that the better way to attack the safety issues, which are mostly at oval tracks is aerodynamically or with the tires, rather than with the engine. I think that if you do it with the engine,

Doug Wendt Photo

Chevrolet's dominance of Indy car racing has led some advertising people to create some rather conceited ad campaigns.

If you altered nothingelse, and you wanted to reduce the speed at an oval significantly, you would have to reduce the engine power a long way. I remember when the super vees used to run on the ovals, they used

Steve Weaver Photo

to run about 180 MPH on 200 horse power.

IICR: If they were to have unlimited boost, could you get over 1000 HPut of an engine?

Morgan: Oh, yes. I don't think that would be a problem at all.

IICR: Why did Ilmor start leasing engines rather than the original plan of having teams buy them outright?

Morgan: The reason is purely the

control that we have. It does involve us with a lot of hassles. But we, nevertheless, think it's well worth while because it allows us to keep a high quality program. We don't want to get in to the situation that the Cosworth DFX program got into in its later days where some teams turned up at races with engines that were in very poor states of rebuild. They used to fail very frequently, which is absolutely not what we want to get in to. We want to make sure that the engines are run properly and also that we don't have a repeat of the engines getting into our cometitors hands, which was an unfortunate set of circumstances.

IICR: Speaking of the incident when Pat Patrick turned over a Chevy to Alfa Romeo for inspection, How much did that hurt Ilmor? I mean, Alfa never really did anything.

Morgan: Well, to be honest, we thought that it would hurt us a lot more than it actually did. But I think that if you look at the Alfa Romeo inlet system, which was one of the obvious features of the engine that you can actually see, it bore a significant similarity to the Chevy after they had the option to look at one of our engines. What other things they used, we don't know. The overall effect on the whole program was

13

that it still didn't make the thing competitive, which we were rather surprised about.

IICR: Are your employees contracted so that they just can't quit and go to work for your competitors? Is there any kind of stipulation that says if they quit, they can't go to work with your competitors for a certain amount of time?

Morgan: Well, we tend to look after our engineers as well as we can. We always believe that the reason that people work here is because they want to work here. I think that once you lose a situation where people have got their mind set that they want to go somewhere else for some particular reason, then they're not going to work well for you if they have their mind on other things. I don't think that there's any real benefit in having long term contracts with people. We spend a lot of time trying to encourage the fact that the company runs as a team. If people no longer feel part of the team, then they clearly need to do whatever they think is best.

IICR: Ok, here's a nosey one, can you give me a ballpark figure on what it costs to develop a modern Indy car engine from start to finish?

Morgan: It is difficult to give you a round figure and it would be misleading to do so. The easy part of developing an engine is to get on to the dyno. The difficulties start then, because that really proves whether you've done a good or a bad job in designing it. You can spend a relatively small amount of money on getting it on the dyno and not do a very good job and then spend an absolute fortune thereafter. Alternately, you can do a really good job on getting it on the dyno and not spend much in development thereafter. We try and always aim towards the latter approach of trying to think of as many problems as possible during the design stage. It does get very expensive when you start doing agressive development with running engines.

IICR: Can you tell me how much a lease program costs?

Morgan: The older style engine costs around $100,000. A lease program, depending on the year, in round terms, it's about $500,000 to lease seven engines excluding rebuilding cost. It's based on the same sort of way if you were leasing a machine tool. It's based on the capital value of the engine and so forth.

IICR: What do you see in the future as far as engine development is concerned? Like in five or ten years?

Morgan: I think that eight cylinders is a good number for a 2.5 liter engine. If the rules were relaxed so that you could use twelve cylinders, then I don't think that would do anything except put the cost up. I think that it really depends on what the rule makers have in mind. Obviously, as the years go by, the engines get better and better. Whether it's an eight cylinder or any other configuration, it will gradually get smaller. It's very interesting to see the difference between the original Indy engine that we designed and what you can do seven years down the road as far as size is concerned and also in improved power.

IICR: Do you and Mario ever look back to the first Chevy and realize how much better the new engine is?

Morgan: I know that Mario certainly does. Particularly last year when Mario designed the Formula One engine. That took a large proportion of his time. When we then went back to look at the Indy car engine, it obviously spawned a lot of thoughts as to improving the various bits and pieces, which suddenly started looking rather large.

IICR: Do you anticipate the new B engine lasting for around seven years like the first design?

Morgan: It's very dependent on what the level of competition is. If some of the Japanese start coming in and producing aggresive engines, then I would imagine the pace of development would have to pick up. It just depends on what it takes to stay winning races.

$\square$

Using racing engines to heat a factory ?

While touring the Ilmor factory, Paul Morgan opens a door revealing a huge square shaped mass with pipes sticking out of it.

"This is our storage tank for the hot water that we use to heat our radiators", he says. Their system uses hot water circulating inside metal radiators which give off heat. After checking into the system, I found it works like this: When an engine runs on the dyno, the engine's cooling system is connected with pumps which lead to the 2,000 gallon storage tank. The heated water is then run through various pipes through to the offices and the blow-heaters in the factory. "That's a great idea, these guys are pretty sharp" I think to myself. "A good one day test of one of our Formula 1 engines will heat the factory for two days" reveals Morgan. The system was conceived by Mario Illian. I found out that, not only is Mr. Illian an outstanding racing engine designer, he can also fall back on a career as a plumber. Illian thought about this long before the factory was built. "I've always thought that it is important to make some kind of contribution to energy savings. We have a well insulated building so the system works quite well. I designed a solar heating system for my parent's house long before getting into motor racing. It took eight months to build and it still works to this day ". Morgan proudly divulges that Ilmor's gas bill is only 100 Pounds per month. Upon a little bit of investigation, I learn that the monthly gas bill for a normal factory the same size as Ilmor is around 800 Pounds. 700 Pounds ($1,260) per month is the monthly dividend of this investment. That's 8,400 Pounds (over $15,000) a year in energy savings! That means the Ilmor is only running at 12 % of the industry normal as far as natural gas consumption. Oddly enough, motor racing is one of the industries where energy consumption is very important. Just think, if Ilmor treated its natural gas consumption the same sort of way as the 1.8 mile per gallon rule that dictates Indy car fuel consumption, they would be getting 14.4 mile per gallon!

COSWORTH

On the day before Halloween,1991, Cosworth made the announcement that it had signed an agreement to supply their advanced new X-B engine to the Newman / Haas and Chip Ganassi racing teams. This announcement surely sent a chill down the spines of Ilmor and Chevrolet. The Cosworth X-B was now at the hands and feet of the hottest driver in the series, young Michael Andretti. Worst of all for Chevy, the name of their arch rival graced the new engines cam covers. It's Ford versus Chevy in America's biggest automotive arena, the PPG Indy Car World series and it's going to be a shoot out for years to come.

It's nice to have the familiar Cosworth name back in the competitive limelight. Cosworth first entered Indy car racing in 1975. Vel's-Parnelli Jones Racing, known as the "Super Team" at the time, bolted a Cosworth DFX into a Formula 1 car that had been modified to USAC specifications. The engine had enough power but the chassis was ill handling and was giving Mario Andretti grey hair. Andretti later abandoned the car during practice at Indianapolis, switching to an old reliable Eagle-Offy (Offenhauser) setup. Cosworth first qualified at Indianapolis in 1976, with Al Unser finishing seventh. Two years later, Unser would use Cosworth power to etch his name on the Borg-Warner trophy for the third time. This was the start of ten consecutive Indy wins and ten National Championships for the British company.

By 1987, the good years were starting to fade. When the Chevy Ilmor was born in 1985, it was the beginning of the end of Cosworth's dominate reign of almost ten seasons. By 1988, Cosworth was fighting back with a short stroke version of the DFX. The DFS became the engine of reality for those teams that were denied the right to the exclusive Chevy. Although the DFS had the ingredients of success, it was later abandoned by those upper eschelon teams who had gained access to the 'red bow tie'. The peak of the DFS project came at the Meadowlands in 1989 when Bobby Rahal and the Kraco team won in the rain. By 1990 Rahal and Kraco had switched to Chevy power and the DFS really didn't have a chance. Sure, "middle of the pack" teams were using them but dreams of another victory seemed as remote as a 10 car pile-up at the start of any given race. The DFS was dying at an early age. Cosworth was down but not out. Cosworth has been developing Formula 1 engines with moderate success. All the while, things were brewing in the Indy car program's design office. Press reports began to reveal that Cosworth was embarking on the design of a new wave of engine technology. This project seemed to be a personal mission for the Cosworth employees, as two of their former buddies (Mario Illian and Paul Morgan) had made it big with their own design, a design that was considered by Cosworth to be contrived while the two were still on the Cosworth payroll.

Cosworth was founded in 1958 when

The Cosworth Racing Division consists of several different buildings.

Keith Duckworth and Michael Costin combined their talents. The two had originally met while attending Imperial College in London. For all of the companies success over the next 30 years, there was once a time when the dream didn't happen. It was late December 1959 and all was not well. The bank manager had refused a line of credit to pay off a $50 telephone bill. Costin and Duckworth were in a tight corner. Being the innovative chaps they were, they were able to master the art of maneuvering out of such unfortunate circumstances.

Today, Cosworth is owned by Vickers P.L.C., an international company based in the U.K. with annual sales of 1.26 billion dollars and over 12,000 employees worldwide. Vicker's other principal activities are Rolls-Royce and Bentley motor cars, Rivapowerboats, armoured fighting vehicles (tanks), medical equipment, marine engineering and superalloys, and precision components for the aerospace and automotive industries. With all of this under their belt, buying a company that produced racing engines must have seemed to be right up their alley.

To the average race fan, the name Cosworth is only regarded as a small company in England that churns out successful racing engines. While the latter is true, the small company image went by the wayside as I approached Cosworth's racing division located on St. James Mill Road in Northampton. First of all, there are buildings with the Cosworth logo on them all over the place. As I walk through the rotating doors of the main lobby, the reception room reveals more. The phones are ringing off the hook as two receptionists field the incoming calls. "I'm Rick Amabile here to see Denise Proctor" I say. "I'll ring her, would you like some tea "? they reply. I'm sitting in the lobby thinking to myself "Why is this place so busy?" A question that is later revealed as I learn that racing engines only make up about 25 percent of Cosworth's total business. The other 75 percent is dedicated to building road car engines for the European market. Both Ford and Mercedes Benz rely on Cosworth to develop engines for passenger car production.

I'm greeted by Denise in the lobby and she leads me to the Formula 1 shop for a brief tour. A walk back to the main lobby and I'm led to the meeting room where so many important meetings are sure to take place. I have arranged a visit with Steve Miller and Malcolm Tyrrell. Miller is the Chief Development Engineer of the Indy car project while Tyrrell is the Project Manager.

IICR: The new Cosworth was very fast out of the box, and it seemed pretty reliable. For a new engine, that's pretty rare. Were you pleasantly surprised by this, do you feel lucky, or was it just a matter of the research that went in to the project? (This question draws a look of amusement from both Miller and Tyrrell)

Malcolm Tyrrell: It wasn't anything to do with luck, it was just that from day one, Steve and I obviously decided that reliability is a very important issue. We're designing a product which has a lot of horse power and is very quick for a short period of time. Durability has played a very key part in the development of the engine.

Steve Miller: There were other factors also. One is just our experience, in the fact that we've designed a lot of racing engines. Ilmor obviously accepted starting a new company as well as designing a new racing engine. Although they (Mario Illian and Paul Morgan) might like to think that they covered all the areas of race engine design before they left Cosworth, then I guess that turned out to be not the case in the very beginning. We've had a stable design team for a long time now. In recent years, we designed the Formula One turbo engine in addition to designing the new road engines which were designed around the racing engines. We're doing the new X-B for Indy racing and now we're working on the V-12 for F-1 racing. We've had a much greater experience in racing engine design

Cosworth's impressive new headquarters building was opened in 1991.

16

Allof this experience is passed among all of the projects so that they can all benefit. Another thing that is in our favor as far as reliability wise, was that the original plan was to go racing in '91. But because of the current state of the market, nobody was prepared to take the risk on board because there was hardly any time to test the engine before the season got started due to the Australian race. We ended up with six to eight extra months to work on the engine than we originally expected.

IICR: How hard was it to entice a team like Newman / Haas Racing who was already winning a lot of races with the Chevy. How hard was it for you to convince them that you could go out right away and run fast?

Miller: We first started talking to Carl Haas about 1989. He kept quite a close watch on the project over a long period of time. Eventually, he had to say "yes" of "no". I admire him for taking the risk. Perhaps it was a shrewd move, we thing that it is. We understand also what the risk is to the Andrettis and to Carl to take that brave step.

IICR: Looking back to 1975, when the DFX was introduced to Indy car racing, and over the 1980's, what is the biggest thing that Cosworth learned about building engines for the Indy car series?

Tyrrell: What you have to remember is that although you mentioned 1975 as when the Cosworth came out, during the formative years of the DFX, Cosworth really sat on the side line watching with keen interest what was going on. We had been approached on several occa

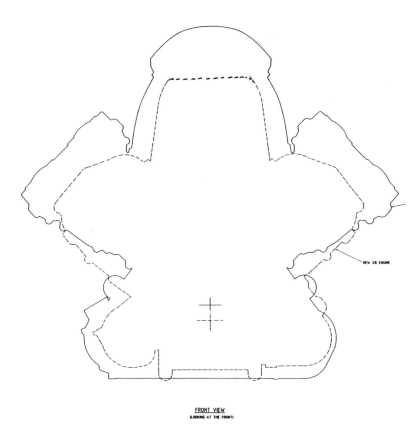

FRONT VIEW
(LOOKING AT THE FRONT)

NEW XB ENGINE

Line Drawing: Cosworth DFS and new Ford-Cosworth XB Indy Car Engines

sions before that and the decision was made not to go in to it full scale, fearing that USAC would ban the engine. It finally took VP Jones (Vel's Parnelli Jones Racing) and McLaren engines to develop some form of specification. It had its moments, but it was fairly unreliable. It was really learing the art of fueling engines to run on methanol.

Miller: One difference was the art of using methanol, one of the others was 500 miles. 500 miles is a long way to run a racing engine flat out. In Formula One, you can actually use a little bit more of a fragile engine. It's much faster than F-1 and you have to be able to finish the race.

Tyrrell: We haven't changed any of our manufacturing processes. Whether it's Indy engines running on methanol or turbocharging, all the things that we learn in F-1 and Indy car racing transfer across.

IICR: What do you think is the better fuel for racing engines to run on, gasoline or methanol?

Miller: The problem in F-1 with gasoline is that although there are

broad rules governing what fuel can be used, teams bend the rule as far as they can. So we're seeing some horrifically expensive fuels, which really don't contribute to the racing. But the whole idea of the motor racing industry is to promote companies products. The drivers go out there and tour for the sponsors really. It hasn't improved the racing at all, and this stuff is like $200 a gallon! You have to do all of your testing with it becuase it influences the engine power so dramatically. It's a result that you can't lay down a specific formula for actual engine fuel. Methanol on the other hand is quite a simple chemical and is easy to police. That's really the over riding advantage of methanol.

IICR: Do you think that the F-1 guys will ever switch over to methanol just in the interest of making things easier and cheaper.

Miller: Unfortunately that would get you in trouble with the sponsorship base. Fuel companies sponsor F-1 so they'll lose some revenue for the series if they go to a single fuel.

IICR: When did the XB engine begin? Did you go to the team owners with blueprints, or was it just an idea?

Miller: Laguna Seca, 1988, was when it all started. The managing director of Cosworth at the time, Richard Bowman, went to the Laguna race at the end of '88. He kind of decided then that we should pro uce a new engine. He ran the idea by the engineers and it was spring 1989 when we started talking about the reality of when, rather than the if, of the project. The design was started in June '89. We first ran the engine on the dyno at the end of July 1990.

IICR: Was this new engine a result of the fact that the revision to the DFX, the DRS wasn't really setting the world on fire? After a few years with that, did you say "hey, we need to start totally new and give Ilmor and Chevy a run for their money?

Miller: We've been trying to do that for a long time. It was always a resource issue.

Tyrrell: I think that the DFS could 've still won races in the right hands. By the time the DFS came along, it started being the wholesale application to the Ilmor and the Chevrolet. It became difficult because everybody in racing wants the newest thing. It became very difficult trying to get anybody interested in doing anything with the DFS. But it was still a reasonably competitive package at the time. Luyendyk very nearly won Michigan with it.

IICR: Rahal did win the Meadowlands with it in 1989.

Tyrrell: To attract a better team, you have to have a new product. There was no way we could get a team to give up an Ilmor to come back to what they saw as a 20 year old engine.

Miller: Also people forget the length of time that this went on. The last three races of '88 was when we first ran the DFS. Michael (Andretti) was pretty fast in those last three races. He won the Marlboro Challenge, was second at Laguna and led the Miami race until the clutch failed. So we're looking at a period from when the DFS was launched to the start of the new engine which was only like nine months. Obviously, it would have been foolish to sustain development on the DFS with the new engine coming along. It wouldn't have made commercial sense or sense in getting the new engine off the ground properly.

The external differences between the 'old' DFS and the new X-B engines are easily apparent. The differences inside the engines are even more considerable.

IICR: Who is the designer of the XB?

Miller: My title is chief development engineer. In doing that, then I'm just the team leader of the engineers involved. Stewart Grove was the designer of the engine.

IICR: What is his background?

Miller: He's previously drawn a lot of the major items for the F-1 V-8. He's been with Cosworth for about five years before he started on the X-B.

IICR: Who is rebuilding the new engines?

Miller: We're doing some in England and some in the U.S., in Torrance, California.

Tyrrell: All development and engineering will be done in England.

IICR: How hard is it to design an engine mechanically keeping in mind the fact that it has to be a stressed part of the car ? Does that limit anything ?

Tyrrell: Most engines, whether they are racing engines or not, are stressed engines.

Miller: I think that since the engine is such a compact load of metal and structurally has to be sound anyway, because there's some terrific loads flying around in it, that the addition of the chassis loads are not really dramatic. I think that it's when people take stock block engines that aren't designed for the loads, like racing engines, is when they get into trouble. The engine is at least five times as stiff as the chassis.

IICR: Has there ever been a concern to add any additional mounting

The new X-B is somewhat sleeker than its predesser, launching a new wave of slimline engine designs.

bolts between the engine and the tub? (there are only six)

Miller: We have some different mountings on the X-B, but it's really a compromise between ease of installation and the ideal areas. A hundred bolts would distribute the load nicely, but we're not allowed that luxury.

IICR: What's harder on engines, road courses or super speedways?

Tyrrell: It's just the sustained high speed of the ovals. We have computor printouts of the engines running 20 laps at a time never dropping below 11,800 RPM. Between 11,800 and 12,100. It's the RPM that kills engines. G forces come into it on where's the oil at any one time. It's just the sustained high en

gine speed, that's why Indy is so difficult.

Miller: It's generally piston fatigue that we're concerned about.

IICR: How hard is it to design the oiling system to make sure that oil gets to all the certain places under high G forces?

Tyrrell: It's just the question that we've got the experience. Lots of people coming in to building race engines are pretty intrigued on where on earth we manage to catch the oil and where it is at any one moment in time.

IICR: How many people are involved in the X-B project.

Miller: We've got about nine engineers. About 24 people that work on the project.

Tyrrell: You shouldn't say that there is 24 total people doing the X-B and that's it. It encompasses the whole of the facility which is a much bigger unit. We have a plant that makes purely racing products that's separate from the road car production factory. The road car production plant is off site in Wellingborough which is about 15 miles away.

IICR: Of all of the areas on the new engine, can you tell me which are the ones that you are concerned with as far as reliability?

Miller: I guess all of them. The thing that makes a new racing engine unreliable is normally a sort of lack of attention to detail. It's normally because somebody hasn't given due consideration to some little detail that should've had more thought put in to it.

Tyrrell: You can have a 50 cent drive fail, which stops the oil from pumping which destroys an engine just as easily as something major failing. It's just attention to detail in all areas.

Miller: I think we can say without any over optimism that there is no scecific item that we're concerned about. If we suffer any early unreliability then it's going to be because there was a lack of specification or something of that nature.

IICR: So would you say that it was just your overall experience in the past at building race engines that sort of dictated that once this thing was done on the drawing board, it was right?

Tyrrell: There's always going to be one or two items that you don't quite get right, otherwise you would design and manufacture the engine and go racing on day one. Take quality issues that need 100 percent detail all the while. Most of the parts are manufactured in-house, but we also have several items that are purchase parts from subcontractors. That's the thing that you have to watch.

Miller: Often it might be the particular way that something assembles. It might be difficult for the guy who puts it together. Although he might have some responsibility if it isn't perfect when it is put together, then some of the responsibility is on the guy who designed it to make sure that it can be assembled. That might also include a piece that's brought in from outside that isn't quite right. A lot of things end up as a combined problem specification.

IICR: Are your engineers contracted

so that they can't be hired away by your competition?

Miller: They could be lured away by our competition, but there are arrangements as far as severance pay. Not every engineer in the place, certainly the more junior ones, aren't contracted so they'd essentially be free to leave if they chose to.

The dyno area is a little larger than Ilmor's, perhaps due to Cosworths extensive Formula One program.

It doesn't tend to happen short of the Ilmor people. They've publicly said that they don't want to get in to the business of creating any salary competition with ourselves. We feel likewise. It's sort of a gentlemen's agreement. It's just good sense that we don't have people constantly hopping from one company to another in the same area. That would just bring the ante up for both of us.

IICR: So you just try to make things nice for your employees so they're happy at Cosworth.

Miller: We try to do that. (laughing)

Tyrrell: It's probably a little bit of a different environment than at a racing car manufacturer where historically there's been a lot of movement of personel. Basically, we're an engineering company. People really aren't in to spending one year here and skipping off and going somewhere else. Also, speaking for myself, I see it as a fairly personal battle. I mean the people up the road that used to work here (Mario Illian

and Paul Morgan) used to work along side of me. Nothing would give me greater pleasure then going out and beating them. They have done a damn good job in the past. It's almost like a football game, it's us versus them. I think a lot of the lads in the X-B department feel the same. It comes down to a fairly personal level. There's been people that have taken a fairly few swipes at us in the past few years.

IICR: How much of its total power capability is the Cosworth running at with the 45 inch rule?

Miller: It depends what you did to the engine really, Rick. I wouldn't like to say what boost we could run at and have the thing still stay in one piece and what power we could achieve.

Tyrrell: Going back to the DRX days, the original boost that we were allowed was 80 inches. Although people were quoting 1000 HP, 850 HP was about the maximum power that we saw. But we only ran the things to 9,000 RPM. Later on in the development with the boost coming down and down and down, we were running at 45 inches and running at 12,000 RPM. At that stage, we were getting in excess of 700 HP. Actually it's a trade off between boost and RPM.

IICR: Is the X-B designed specifically for the 45 inch rule area?

Miller: A little but not very much. Compression ratio and things like that. If the boost were to become unlimited, we would have probably designed a different engine. It would have a longer stroke and smaller valves and things like that. It was designed for a low boost. As far as 45 inches specifically, I don't think you can consider that.

IICR: Cosworth had a pretty close call when there was talk of switching to 3.5 liter engines. All of your work and investment would have gone

A technician programs the various 'face' and 'bore' settings on the Mazatrol machine. Like other manufacturers, all machining is conducted by computer commands.

down the drain. That must have been....

Tyrrell: Of concern!

IICR: Yeah, that would have been a disaster for you. What kind of lobbying was done to save the engine?

Tyrrell: It wasn't only to save the engine but to explain that the 3.5 liter rule was going to be extremely expensive. A lot of people think that the 3.5 liter rule would have been very, very cheap, but in fact the reverse is the case.

Miller: After talking to people, what I imagine happened was that the 3.5 liter brigade went and asked all the manufacturers that if they were going to enter Indy car racing, would they prefer to have a 2.65 turbocharged formula, or a 3.5 liter naturally aspirated formula? Of course, by in large, everybody, with the exception of Ilmor and ourselves, said 3.5 liters. But I don't think they actually asked the question, which should have been asked, that if we made the formula 3.5 liters, would you go Indy car racing? If you asked anybody who is involved in Formula One or Group C what engine rules they wanted, they're going to say 3.5 liters, because they already have

Although competitive given the right team, the Cosworth DFS turned out to be a bad investment for the company.

3.5 liter engines! It doesn't mean that they're going to go Indy racing. That's the step that was never taken. So it was quite easy to quote big manufacturers as saying we would prefer 3.5 liter engines at Indy. Of course, they would prefer 3.5 liters, but that doesn't mean that they are going to go Indy car racing. We did all the lobbying that we could do and luckily good sense has prevailed.

IICR: Did you guys fly over to the States and have a big lengthy discussion with Tony George about this?

Miller: No, we didn't. I guess what was really played out with the 3.5 liter thing was that the Speedway was quickly becoming pals with F-1. I think that they found that wasn't quite as easy as it first appeared.

Tyrrell: There were some fairly sweeping statements

made without consultation. It was a fairly swift rift between the two parties.

IICR: Ok, getting away from that, do you do all of your own castings?

Miller: We cast all of the major items at our plant in Worcester.

IICR: Can you tell me about how many hours it takes to cast, machine and assemble to get the X-B to the final product?

Tyrrell: We could probably tell you if you come back in three days time!

Miller: How many total man hours?

Tyrrell: I think that we estimated that it takes about 40 hours to machine a block. It's fairly difficult to estimate total hours. A cylinder head doesn't just go on to a machine and bang, it's done. In the old days, a head was picked up and one face was done, then it had to go on to another jig to another machine and sent to another face to be done. Nowadays, a lot of the machining gets done on a single machine.

Miller: You've got to be looking at something like a thousand hours of labor in an engine.

IICR: If everything goes right with the X-B, will you make it available to any team that wants it in the future?

Miller: We can only grow at a rate which is sensible for us. We certainly don't want to trip over ourselves by trying to supply every customer who may come knocking on our door. We will attemp to sup

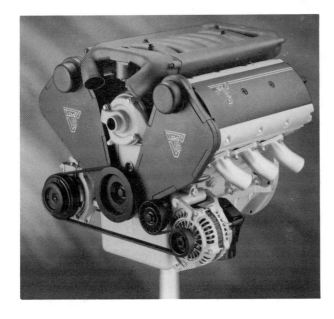

Cosworth regularly transfers its racing technology into road car engines. Here is the new MBA 2.5 liter V-6 concept engine, unvailed in early 1991.

ply as many customers that is sensible to do. Realistically, that's not going to be any more than eight cars

Tyrrell: We want to supply as many cars as is sensible because that's our income.

IICR: Do you think that Ford and Cosworth might fall into the same political circumstances as Ilmor and Chevrolet as far as having the upper hand on who gets a competitive engine?

Miller: No. The reason for saying that is because we are an independent organization who are in charge of distributing the engine. It had become a regular pilgrimage in Indy car racing for teams to go and see Roger Penske during the last 1/3 of the season and find out if they could have a Chevy for the following season. We're not in a position and never want to end up in that position. We don't want to maintain the power base in the sport where we're in charge of dishing out the premier engine.

We don't want to maintain the power base in the sport where we're in charge of dishing out the premier engine.

IICR: Did Cosworth basically finance the design and construction of the X-B out of its own pocket?

Miller: Yes, it was our initiative. But I think that we talked to Ford during the whole time that the engine was being designed and its initial running. In the end, it was the same stance that the teams were in to say "yes" or "no". For them it was also a brave step to get back involved with Indy car racing. Also with the state of the auto market in the U.S., it was a brave step financially. So it had to be something that we had a great deal of confidence in.

IICR: In the early days of the project, did you approach any other major car companies?

Miller: No. We really weren't in a position to pursue any other manufacturers as a sponsor because of our close relationship with Ford on a number of topics, both the road engine projects and Formula One.

IICR: Can you tell me about how much it costs to develop the modern racing engine to get it on to the dyno? (This one as expected brings on confidential laughter into the room) Any round figures?

Miller: If you've got an established company (like Cosworth) it costs surprisingly little money to produce the first prototype engine. It's certainly less than five million dollars. Where the real escalation in money comes is when you start producing several engines that you have to go run in a car. You have to support the cost of producing the engine and the services, then by the time it gets on the track, any updates or modifications become quite expensive because you have a lot of engines about. To produce three or four prototypes and do some dyno testing is quite inexpensive. To go racing, that's where the real money comes in.

IICR: Is the X-B program a purchase or a lease program?

Tyrrell: It's a lease program.

IICR: Why is this different than in the past with your purchase program?

Tyrrell: Because we've sold off our technology in the past. We want to keep our technology in-house obviously. That's the way it is in motor racing generally. Engine makers started leasing engines years and

Ironically, Al Unser, Sr. gave the 'old style' DFX its first and last victories at Indianapolis. Here, 'Big Al' is on the way to winning the big number four in 1987.

Doug Wendt Photo

years ago in Formula 3000 and F-1. It just seems to be the trend. I think that the teams think that it's a better deal because they won't end up with engines that are probably going to be obsolete over time.

Miller: It does have its drawbacks for us. It's pretty easy for teams to ditch us at the end of the year. They have no capitol. They can just turn their head and leave.

IICR: How much does it cost for a lease program?

Miller: We're really not in a position to say until the end of the 1992 season. The original agreement with Newman / Haas and Ganassi Racing in starting this thing out, we both shared some of the risk of racing the engine in the first year, financial risk. So what the price tag will be at the end of the 1992 season when we're looking at picking teams up for '93 will be determined then.

IICR: Did you work pretty closely with Lola Cars in the design of the Ford X-B ?

Tyrrell: Yes, we actually have a scale model of the Lola. We have a very good relationship with them. It was the same with March in the old days. The whole essence is the total package. You can't just say "here's the engine, get on with it". Lola of course built a special car for the X-B.

IICR: When was the DFX program retired? How many were built during the 70's and 80's?

Miller: I guess the DFX program was stopped when the DFS project was initiated in late '88, early '89.

Tyrrell: There were actually 370 DFX, stroke DFS, because we crossed over. But in addition to that, the kits that we supplied to teams, they didn't have an engine number, they had a kit number. So you probably have to add another 160 to 200 on to that. I can't give you a definite figure, but it's well over 550. That's not suggesting that there still are 550 engines still around because some were blown or are in pieces.

IICR: I think that you can buy a used Cossie for under $5,000. People still want them for their vintage cars, etc.

IICR: Do you ever seek patents on any of your technology?

Miller: Generally not for racing, because it moves too quickly. It's difficult to police and almost impossible to enforce a case. We do seek patents on our road engines.

Tyrrell: Vickers (Cosworth's parent company) has their own patent department, so it makes it easy.

IICR: What do you think of these new synthetic oils being used in your engines?

Tyrrell: We've tried to conduct some

Michael Andretti, Cosworths best chances of winning with the X-B.

tests to see if there's anything in it as far as extra horsepower. We've found that there is very little difference, sometimes not any difference.

Miller: I guess that you could say that there is a very small benefit performance wise.

IICR: How many times can you overhaul an engine?

Tyrrell: It's difficult to say because engines vary. 2,500 to 3,000 miles, something like that. Maybe six to ten overhauls.

IICR: If you were to take a Cosworth and only run it 60 MPH, could you run that engine just like a normal road engine?

Miller: I guess that if you put one in a car and reved it to only 8,000 RPMs, it wouldn't surprise me if you could get 30,000 miles without hav

ing any trouble at all.

IICR: How many MPH is 8,000 RPMs?

Miller: If you talked in horsepower terms that's probably 500 HP at 45 inches.

IICR: Wrapping things up, how many trips to the States will you make per season? Do you get used to all of the traveling?

Miller: Typically, I'll make between twelve and fourteen trips per year. Malcolm and I overlap job responsibilities considerably. The good side to that is that we both share the traveling. Otherwise, it would probably kill us to fly to every race. I mean, we have to accomplish things back here in the mean time.

Tyrrell: There's sixteen races a year to start with, divided by two, that's eight races each, plus two tests per month. That adds up to about twelve to fourteen trips each.

IICR: At least you're cleaning up in frequent flyer milage!

Miller: It does build up over the weeks during the season. When I've done a lot of traveling to the States, my sleep patterns get permanately adjusted. I wake up in the middle of the night when I shouldn't. You get this fatigue that builds up.

Tyrrell: You never really get used to the traveling. You just sort of sit there for eleven hours! Half way through, you've had all your food and you've watched the movie and there's still another five hours to go! You have to say to yourself "well it's eleven hours and I have to relax". I could never sleep on a plane initially. One of the benefits about the testing routine is that you're up at five in the morning, you're at the track by six thirty or seven. It's pretty intense even when the car's not running. You sometimes finish at eleven o'clock at night on a bad day, seven o'clock on a good day. That's sort of a typical day. So when you get on to the airplane to come back home, you really don't have that much problem sleeping!

LOLA CARS LTD

Glebe Road, St. Peter's Hill, Huntingdon
Cambridgeshire PE18 7DS, England
Telephone 44-(0)480-451301
Fax 44-(0)480-456722   Telex 32192

WINNER
1990

"England is the Silicon Valley of motor racing", mentions Colin Whittamore as we walk across the assembly floor of Lola Cars. This casual statement turns out to be the most logical statement I've heard concerning the dominance of the

Lola Cars as it was in 1988.

British racing industry.

Once again I find myself in the back of a cab traveling through downtown Huntingdon. "Take me to the Lola factory on Glebe road and St. Pertershill" I said and made the mistake of assuming that the driver knew where the worlds largest race car manufacturer hung its shingle. After five minutes of minor panic, we finally found the right street. "It's on this road, I was here back in '88". Since I had last paid a visit to Lola, I had heard that they had done some expanding.

Rightly so, over the past 35 years Lola has established itself as THE builder of successful racing cars. The company had been founded by Eric Broadley in 1957. Lola first came to Indy car racing in 1965, perhaps to try to imitate Colin Chapman's

success with the Lotus revolution. The following year Graham Hill won the 500 at the controls of a Lola T-90. By 1968, the clever Broadley had conceived a four wheel drive transmission design under the Hewland banner. A year later, Al Unser finished third at Indy in a Lola T-152- four wheel drive. The transmission was successful, so much so that it was later banned. "Big Al", who was known as

Opened in 1991, the new addition mainly consists of administrative offices.

simply "Al", Bobby's brother at the time, would again drive a Lola at Indianapolis, but this time it is 1978. This would be Al Unser's big year. After winning Indy in a T500, Unser scored again in the second 500 miler at Pocono in late June, but three was his lucky number in '78. Al and Lola would go on to win the first ever triple crown at Ontario, a place that would see

the wrecking ball only two years later. Oddly enough, after such a successful year, Lola packed up and left the Indy car scene.

This leads us to 1983, the year that would mark the third time around for Lola Cars Ltd.. Things were a little ragged at first, but chief engineer Broadley was able to sort things out. A typical scene during May 1983 in Gasoline Alley would see a tired Broadley making his was back and forth between the Newman / Haas garage and the garage of another pioneering customer, AMI Racing. By the end of the 1983, Mario Andretti had won twice , with three second and one third place finish. At the end of 1984 Andretti won the Championship. By 1985 it was March vs. Lola, engaging in battle on Sunday afternoons all across North America. That year Lola ended up selling 22 T-900 chassis. The success of the March 85C would see Lola's order list reduced to 15 the following year. 1987 would be a strange year for both British manufacturerers due to Goodyears switch to radials for the

The reception area.

Rick Amabile Photo

Rick Amabile Photo

first time at Indianapolis. You may remember 1987 as the year that drivers were wadding up cars right and left, especially at Indianapolis. Nonetheless, Lola went on to win the Championship with Bobby Rahal. The significance for Lola was the fact that Rahal and TrueSports were a March account in 1986 and although they won Indy and the Championship, took their business elsewhere. 1988, another successful year for Lola. The T-88 turns out to be one of the better cars financially, tallying 29 cars. But Lola hadn't peaked yet. 1990 Indy winner Arie Luyendyk would give Lola yet another trophy, but amazingly enough it was only the third time Lola had won the big one after so many successful years that preceeded it. 1991 was the year that the molds were worn out. 35 Indy cars were built, not counting the many spare parts that went out with them. Over 14 million American dollars went through the Lola bank account that fiscal year. I notice that all of the wealth has had a certain effect on the facility when we finally make our way into the Lola parking lot. "Looks like they put some money back into the place" I think to myself as I pay the driver. In its present form the place looks like it could double for some of the corporate offices in the Fortune 500. Lola Cars is a Fortune 500 company of a different sort, they make a fortune building cars for the 500- the Indy 500.

I'm met in the lobby by a dapper Colin Whittamore, who is the project co-ordinator for Lola. Whittamore once worked for British Leyland before joining Lola Cars two years ago.

IICR: First off, how many people does Lola now employ, total?

Colin Whittamore: We currently have 110. It's a little bit transient because in the summer we have less than in the winter. We probably lose about 20 people during the summer months.

IICR: Where do those people go?

Whittamore: Generally, they go to race teams. They normally come back to us for winter work in the assembly shop.

IICR: How many people are on the design staff?

Whittamore: About 27 people. That includes all the various projects. We have three projects: Indy cars, F-3000 and Group C sports cars. Each project has its own design leader (Bruce Ashmore is the leader of the Indy car project). Then they have four or five detail draftsmen below them.

IICR: How many assemblers are there that produce Indy cars? How many machinists and fabricators?

Whittamore: There are five assemblers. There are fifteen machinists

The spacious drawing office is the birth place of race winning designs.

The state of the art CAD/CAM office.

and about the same number of fabricators. In addition, there are three guys who assemble the tubs.

IICR: Has it ever been estimated how many hours it takes to build a Lola?

Whittamore: No, it hasn't because the machine and fabrication work are totally separate. The actual assembly time is just over two

hundred hours.

IICR: What sort of weekly time period is there from start to finish?

Whittamore: There's no set finish time of the design, it's not like the design gets finished and the car gets started, things overlap. Once the thing is up and running, it's about two months from the time the first tub gets assembled till it's out the door. In the middle of production, when we actually have all of the parts in stock, about three weeks.

IICR: What if a team writes a car off early in the season, like at Australia or Long Beach or Phoenix?

A technician reviews a Formula One design.

Rick Amabile Photo

Rick Amabile Photo

Whittamore: In that sort of situation, probably two weeks because we have all of the parts on the shelf by then. By that time we don't have to worry about designing any parts.

IICR: How many 1992 Lolas were sold ? How many did you sell in '91?

Whittamore: 22 cars were sold initially. Usually as the season goes on a few more are sold because of crashes and so forth. 37 cars were sold in 1991 throughout the year.

IICR: As the largest Indy car manufacturer, what sort of design compromises do you have to meet to satisfy your customers? Does technology get watered down any when you go into big production?

Whittamore: Not really, because we are responsive to the individuals needs. For example, take the Cosworth X-B, we responded to that by redesigning certain areas to accomodate the different engine. It's practically different for the others from the driver backwards. Because the X-B has advantages that we can exploit, we use them. The Buick chassis, that's also a special build, but it's not quite as different from the standard Ilmor chassis. We're not so big that we act like Henry Ford and just churn them out. We will respond to what individual teams require within certain parameters. We also have a wide cockpit option.

IICR: When Lola designs a car, what size driver do you basically take into consideration?

Whittamore: Drivers are starting to get a little bit bigger. A couple years ago, the driver had to be about five foot six! But now the cockpits are starting to get a little bigger. I think that what happened was that the whole industry assumed that the driver was smaller, sort of five foot six and very lean. It got to the stage where a driver who is average sized, five foot eight and upward, just wasn't comfortable in the car.

IICR: Does that present big problems when you try to get the steering box from out of the driver's shins?

Whittamore: Yes, it can be a problem for Bruce and the boys.

IICR: If CART- INDY CARS ever decided to get rid of on-board computors in the interest of reducing costs, would Lola object?

Whittamore: We designed our own system in 1992, so it would hurt us.

IICR: Why did Lola do that?

Lola founder, Eric Broadley (L) discusses business with Kraco owner Maury Kraines.

Whittamore: We weren't specifically happy with the collaboration with P i Research. We only had a one year exclusive deal with them anyway, with the "Black Box". We just felt that we would have more control over it if it were designed in-house. We don't actually manufacture it in-house, we just design it. It was designed by Paul Russell. (As we're discussing this matter, Whittamore sees Steve Bunkhall walking down the hall and asks him to join our conversation. Bunkhall is the intelligent Instrumentation product manager for Lola. Along with Paul Russell is responsible for the Lola "Traktel" instrumentation system.)

Steve Bunkhall: A ban would hurt us at the moment because we spent some money developing the system. If they (CART INDY CARS) made a decision to do it across the board and nobody had access, then I guess that everybody's in the same boat.

IICR: There's just a trend in America where they're starting to look at things to control the outrageous costs. I don't think they want to do anything half-assed, they just want to control costs. Things that you don't need for competitive racing.

Bunkhall: I think that they're taking a fairly sensible view on things like active suspension and semi-automatic gear boxes. Those are going to cost you a lot of money. The data loggers and the dash displays aren't really upping the ante that much.

IICR: Is that equipment going to get any cheaper in time, sort of like the way that personal computors have gone down?

Bunkhall: The problem we have is that the volume that we manufacture is too small to really achieve that kind of price break. They could get cheaper if we started knocking out ten thousand units, but that's not going to happen.

IICR: Is that compatible with any

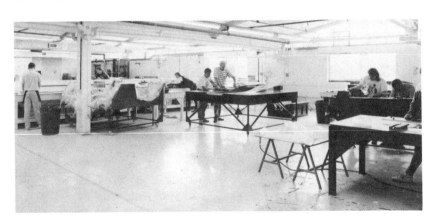

The composite shop, located accross the road from the main building.

other racing cars ?

Bunkhall: The thing that we've designed is designed to go across the board. We tailor it for a particular type of car. It's just a matter of fitting it to the particular installation. These systems are expensive, but you don't have to buy a new system every year. You can probably use it for two or three years at least.

Whittamore: We haven't built in obsolescence into the system, the thing can be upgraded. It's modular, you can even interact it with other systems. It's not designed so that once you have it for a year it's obsolete.

IICR: So you can upgrade the system with different software?

Bunkhall: That's right. Three years a go when the system was new, I think that not a lot of people were fairly educated about the thing. But they're much more tuned in now to using the stuff and seeing what it can do. I think that they want to see it last three years now. I think that it's become so much a part of racing now that to go out without it would be a major step backwards. The information that you gain from it is invaluable. It's good for us because it helps us build better cars, safer cars. Instead of having to guess what loads the suspension experiences, you can actually measure it with the system, so you know what specific loads there are. Plus if there is a crash, the unit is usually undamaged. If the system does fail, it doesn't put the driver in any danger.

IICR: Is (Lola founder) Eric Broadley still active in the company? Or is he just a so-called consultant?

Whittamore: He is still very active. He comes in every day. He's still very much a part of the design staff.(Half way through our conversation Mike Blanchet, Lola's managing director drops by and we are introduced.)

IICR: What is the price of the 1992 Lola Indy car ?

Mike Blanchet: The list price landed in the States of the Chevy car is $360,000. That is based on an exchange rate of 1.7 (Dollars to British Pounds) but now (Spring 1992) the exchange rate is 1.8, so it's a little higher ($381,000). That's the price with the road course set up.

IICR: How much is the oval set-up ?

Blanchet: We really work hard on that up until the last minute to get the maximum out of it. With the oval kit

there is a side-pod kit that is optional, without that, the kit is $40,000 to $50,000. With the optional side-pods, it's a b o u t $70,000. The Buick cars are $330,000 and they come oin s p e e d w a y trim only. The reason that the Buick chassis is less expensive than the Chevy is that basically Buick has helped subsidize the cost of design and tooling involved in making it a special Buick car. We felt it was only reasonable that we should not pass on the extra cost on to the customers. But no one paid us to do the Chevy installation, we had to do all that ourselves. That's why it's a little more expensive. The Cosworth X-B car is also being funded entirely by us. An X-B car is more expensive than the standard car for that reason. We hope that we can get a return on the X-B car in the future when more engines b e c o m e available. If e v e r y t h i n g goes well with the X-B, and we expect that it will, more teams will get them in '93 and we will get our return then.

IICR: So it's just like any other business where an investment may take a couple of years to start paying off.

A '92 chassis being assembled piece by piece. This is the cockpit area lower section. The upper half is sitting on the floor.

The dash and steering wheel are mounted on the bulkhead in the center of the photo.

The transmission assembly area.

Rick Amabile Photo

Blanchet: Yes. It's difficult with race cars because you change them so much. The '92 car is 80 percent new over the '91 model. Normally, you have to work on advertising your design too over the one year. In the case of the X-B, it's a very

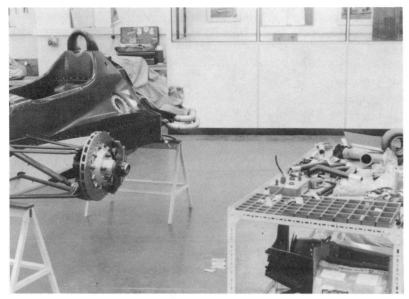

When an order is received, the parts department pulls all parts needed to build a car, then puts them on a cart and wheels them out to the shop floor where the assemblers take over.

advanced design and because we're really looking at quite a new family of engines. We feel that what we're learning this year, we'll get a return on in the future. Perhaps that will be over a two or three year period. I must say that that's fairly unusual because normally with Indy cars we have to reckon that we would have to get all of our return back in one year, because the designs change so much from year to year. Sports cars are different, like the Group C car we're doing again, we expect to get our return over a two to three year period. Initially, you've got to be looking at something like a million pounds ($1,800,000) in design tooling, so it's very difficult to make that up in one year considering the amount of sales that we're likely to make. Sports cars are a bit different. They tend to have a longer life because drivers aren't so much looking for the last tenth of a second in track performance as having a competitive overall package that's reliable, easy to maintain as well as being fast. In Indy cars and Formula 3000 (The next step before Formula One) the thing that matters is having that little extra bit of competitive edge. To do that we have to make enormous changes every year.

IICR: Why was the decision to re-enter Indy car racing in 1983 made then and not earlier?

Blanchet: I guess it was because Carl Haas sold the idea to us. He wanted to go Indy car racing because the Can Am series had gone flat. We had a successful association with Carl back in 1978, and the feeling was that the Indy car series, with CART having taken over, was going to take off and be strong. Although the decision was made very late and therefore we struggled a bit because the car was made in a hurry, we still won races in the first year. The whole thing just developed from there. But I guess it's because Carl made a good case for us to do it.

IICR: Didn't you guys just look at what was happening to March Engineering and decide that you should get in on the action?

Blanchet: It had not escaped our notice! We felt the time was right for someone to go in there and give them a bit of competition.

IICR: Lola does all of its wind tunnel testing at the Cranfield Institute. Is it cheaper to do this rather than build your own wind tunnel?

Blanchet: Yes, but there are also a couple of other factors. It's a very good tunnel. We know it very well now. Bear in mind that although we hire the tunnel, all of the instrumen-

tation in it is ours that we've developed and were designed for that tunnel. The high speed moving ground, we've had a lot of input into. We're continually updating and improving. In that respect, it's like having our own tunnel. To build a tunnel from scratch is very expensive, and you can easily build in some problems. It's a bit of a black art, wind tunnels are.

IICR: I've heard that it takes like two or three years to get a tunnel where everything is just right.

Blanchet: Yes, many people have had a lot of problems in F-1 and so forth. They'll build a brand new tunnel and it's taken eighteen months to two years to actually be able to get good, repeatable results in it. We can't afford to have that kind of gap. It's not to say that we won't do it. We do look at it regularly and it could well be that in the future we will build our own tunnel. At the moment, we're very happy with Cranfield. I think that our results prove that it's given us the right kind of information. We're continually updating and improving it. I guess that if it gets to a stage where if the only way forward is to actually start from scratch, then we will probably build our own tunnel. But while we can use Cranfield effectively and keep getting the kind of information that we need, there's no real reason to change. You can spend a couple of million pounds doing something else.

IICR: So if it ain't broke, don't fix it.

Blanchet: That's right. If something's working well leave it alone. That's not to say that you don't parallel it with other alternatives so that if one satisfaction with that set up starts to fall off, you're already down the road to doing something else. You've got to be ahead of any problems. We make sure to go and look at other ideal wind tunnels when they're available to make sure that we're not falling behind in any way. Judging by what we see, we feel that our set up is probably better than most of them.

IICR: Although Carl Haas is your North American distributor, has Lola ever considered building a factory in America?

Blanchet: Carl's our distributor, but wouldn't in any way prevent us setting up a manufacturing operation in the States. It's something that we think about quite often. In many ways, a lot of manufacturing is actually cheaper in the States then it is over here. It's changed totally in the last ten to fifteen years. It used to be the exact reverse. One of the problems though is that the States is a great place for making things in huge quantities. The production engineering is very good. But when it comes to making small quantities, which is what we're really talking about, highly specialized, it's more difficult to find the sort of places and the back-up of supplies that you need in order to do that. England being very small and compact and having a long history of race car manufacturing, everybody's within sort of a hundred to a hundred and fifty miles of each other. It's very easy to get things done quickly. It's more difficult in the States. But I could quite foresee a situation in the near future where we do open a kind of satellite operation in the States to maybe carry out repair and manufacture. It's something that we keep looking at and maybe we'll do.

IICR: Does the lower labor cost in England play a major factor in this consideration? I mean, you can stay in England and be more competitive

The autoclave is where all carbon fiber pieces are cured. Between 10 and 15 items are cured at once, including two Indy car 'tubs'. Curing time is four hours.

price wise.

Blanchet: Yes, but that gap is diminishing. In some areas labor is actually cheaper in the States. The sort of highly specialized labor that we need is quite high in England. Of course, you've got a lot of people at the moment in the automobile and aerospace fields who are out of work and looking hard for jobs. We can get very competitive quotes as a result. The cutback in the defense program is going to have an awful

effect with a lot of aerospace subcontractors. Those are the sort of people that we're talking about. Of course, if you manufacture in the States you avoid the freight and import costs to send the goods to America. Against that, we have to make sure that this place is kept busy all the time because the overhead is very high. The biggest factor is the control. We control quality extremely tightly here. It's not that you couldn't do that in the States, but it adds another dimension of control and management. It's very easy to get fragmented and then you're in trouble. At the moment we run a fairly tight ship and that's why we're able to do what we do.

IICR: Does the weak American dollar give you guys a bum rap?

Blanchet: Sure, that's the problem. It's something that we can do nothing about. We try to encourage customers to commit ahead. If at the time we're making the deal the exchange rate is reasonably low, either they buy British pounds forward or we would sell dollars forward on their behalf. So we can, if we shake hands on the deal, agree to

The final assembly area. Race teams usually ship an engine over and have the car built around it.

29

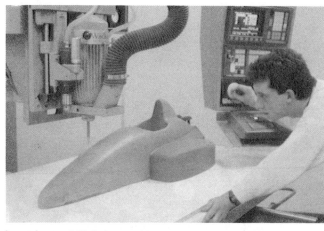
A wooden model is being machined for wind tunnel testing. This is a 1/3 scale Formula One car.

a fixed price at whatever stage the dollar is vs the pound. To some extent we can overcome the problem, but not totally. Obviously the customer then has to take the risk that in fact the exchange rate may be better than the rate he's agreed to when the cars are actually delivered. That's the risk you take.

IICR: Sometimes one of your customers, Dick Simon pulled this in late 1991, complain about the lack of technical support given his team by Lola. Then they issue press statements that they are considering a move to a different manufacturer. How do you keep everybody happy? Does the squeaky wheel get the grease in that respect?

Blanchet: I've got to be honest, there's an element of that, sure. There is a limit to how much we can do. We can't have a team of twenty engineers that we use just sending out to customers. Obviously, part of the fact is that the cost would be prohibitive, we probably couldn't find twenty guys good enough to do that at any given time. In Dick's case, I think he had a fair point, which he made fairly strongly. We covered him. He asked for, and we got a an engineer specifically for him. We hired John Bright, who is employed by us, but assigned to Dick Simon's team. To be fair to us, I think it's fair to say also that Dick had not put in place a proper engineering structure within his team that would have enabled us to work with him the way we're doing now, until now. Dick

realized that. In all credit to the guy, he now has a very strong engineering team. It's pretty well handled now and we did respond to Dick's complaint. Prior to that, one of the problems was that Dick was doing a pretty good imitation of a one-armed paper hanger. He was running his team as a one man band with a few guys who weren't really qualified to engineer the cars. It was a bit of a screw up. It's very difficult to work with that because you can spend a lot of time and effort and you get absolutely nowhere. Dick has seen that and responded to that. He's put a structure in place for the first time which should make the team very competitive.

IICR: Since you have an engineer on Dick Simon's team, is that sort of like a separate test team away from Newman / Haas Racing?

Blanchet: Yeah sure. We work closely with Newman / Haas, Bruce Ashmore in particular, and they are, if you like, our works team. Their cars, contrary to what a lot of people believe, have never been different in any fundamental way from the other customer cars. Newman/Haas does lot of their own development because they have the facilities and resources to do it. We try out our ideas with Newman / Haas because they are willing to spend the money to test them. Our agreement is that those ideas are then passed on to the customers in due time. With Newman / Haas running the Cosworth X-B program, the cars are quite a lot different from the Chevy car. In 1992, we felt the need to work closely with some Chevy teams of which Dick Simon is one, to actually have an engineering input and feedback. We don't want to neglect the Chevy customers in way, shape, or form because that is our call business. We have engineers like John Travis and John Bright who are specifically on those programs.

IICR: In Indy car racing there is always cycles where certain maunfacurers are dominant. Dan Gurney's Eagles were big in the 1970's, Penske was big in the late '70 and early '80s, before coming back in 1988, March was huge from 1982 thru 1988. I look around at this beautiful new facility and wonder

The underside of a car shows aerodynamic 'fences' which are used to fine tune ground effects. These tunnels produce enough downforce to make a car stick to a ceiling at 200 MPH.

Rick Amabile Photo

what Lola does to ensure that they don't go by the wayside the way March did. How do you try and prevent that kind of fall from competitiveness? (This one draws an amusing expression from both Blanchet and Whittamore)

Blanchet: I think that you have to realize there's a bit of a different philosophy in this company then there was in March. This company is very much engineering laid. It stems directly from the man at the top, in our case Eric Broadley. Eric is an engineer first and foremost and his buzz is in coming up with ideas that work and win races. Yes, sure the company's got to be profitable. If you're not profitable you can't invest in equipment, machinery and people. You can't get the job done. First and foremost, we are an engineering oriented company. March I think was much more marketing oriented. The idea was turn a dollar. Sometimes the quality and performance took a second place from doing a very good sales job. I think that caught up to them eventually. Those things always do catch up with you. We do genuinely try and produce the best possble product that we can. That can sound like a bit of bullshit, you can take it like that if you wish, but that is the fact. We obviously keep a close commercial eye on the situation because if you can't make money, you can't do the rest of it. We figure that at the end of the day, if we can't guarantee competitiveness, we can do our utmost to try and make the cars competitive by having good engineers and good facilities. You can guarantee good quality and good service. If you do that, I think that you do get a strong customer loyalty.

IICR: How much does the customer have to absorb when there are fewer cars sold than the previous year. In 1991 you sold 35 cars and 25 in 1992, do you just up the price per car to make up for the development costs?

Blanchet: Yes, it has an effect in price. Like I mentioned, you really have to advertise the design and tooling costs over a one year period. So it must have an effect. It's difficult because we really have to predict that in advance. We set the price of the cars long before: A, what they actually cost, i.e. before they are

Bob Ellis Photo

One of the problem areas of modern Indy car design is having the wheel and suspension parts press their way into the cockpit just after impact. Depending on the angle of impact, sometimes the wheel dosnt have time to escape and can cause considerable injury. The situation is similar to the way a football player can land on a football and have the ball itself cause injury. This 1991 Indy 500 accident happened when Roberto Guerrero and Kevin Cogan tangled going into turn one. Having similar impacts, Guerrero (top) was lucky that the wheel didn't come into the cockpit. Cogan's right front wheel gets pinned between the wall and the cockpit, causing considerable injury. Guerrero walked away from the crash.

Bob Ellis Photo

built; and B, before knowing exactly how many we are going to sell. We kind of get a feel for it. There is some relationship, sure. The more we build, the cheaper it becomes to build each car. We pass that on probably more in the spare parts prices than in the car's price. In 1992, we made a very serious effort to get spare parts prices down. That's one area where I think we have been open to criticism. In the last couple of years, the spares prices have become too high. Both Carl Haas and ourselves, after a lot of discussion, have made a very serious attempt to actually reduce spares prices. In many cases, the cost of spares in 1992 are lower than they were in 1991, even allowing for the cost of inflation built in. We've been able to do this by cutting our margins, by making bigger batches and by making them earlier so that we can ship a lot of spares out in one load to Carl at the start of the season which saves a lot of freight and duty. We've also invested quite a lot in new manufacturing techniques. Basically we both cut our margins on the basis that we understand that in a recession people have got limited budgets . We have to respond to that. We sell cars to Carl Haas and the duty, freight and insurance is his responsibility. That gets included in the landing price of the car in the States.

IICR: So when you sell a car to Carl, it's just like when GM of Ford sell cars to a dealership, then the dealership makes a certain markup?

Blanchet: That's right, it's basically similar. The important thing to the customer is to have a price that includes everything. They don't want to get bills for insurance or freight, so the landing price includes all of that.

IICR: I'm sure that when teams like TrueSports and Galles / Kraco go and build their own cars Lola has to be very concerned. Those two teams alone used to account for seven or eight car sales per year that are a loss to your annual revenue.

Steve Weaver Photo

A tribute to Lola's safety record has been displayed on a couple of occasions by Jim Crawford. In 1989, Crawford sailed into the turn three concrete at 220 MPH. In 1990, Crawford gets airborne after the car runs over its own rear wheel after initial impact. Jim walked away in both cases.

Bob Ellis Photo

Blanchet: Yes, sure, but then we don't expect to have a divine right to a have a monopoly of the Indy car market. Competition is good, it's healthy. We never underestimate anybody. Anybody who starts building their own car is a concern to us. Our argument is that we just have to make sure we keep beating other teams. As long as our cars are winning, people will keep buying them. It's really as pure and simple as that.

Galmer Engineering

Art Flores Photo

Alan Mertens, the chief design engineer for Galmer Engineering seems to be one tired camper. For the last year and a half, Mertens has been working all hours and wearing several hats in the design and reality of the first Galmer Indy car. Following in racing tradition, Galmer is a com-

Halliday (now the chief designer at TrueSports) to build its own car. One single Kraco car was built but the project got caught up in politics when Kraco became the official "works" team for March Engineering in 1986. The Kraco chassis showed promise in testing but was never

panies of Lola and Penske Cars. Although the work force is small, and there really could be more money floating around, Galmer is comprised of people who seem hellbent to succeed.

Rick Amabile Photo

The Bicester town center is typical of any small village in England.

bination of the surnames of the companies founders, Rick Galles and Alan Mertens. In 1988, Galles hired March refugee Mertens to help improve on the already successful March 88C. The idea seemed perfect. Now the team had access to one of the chief idea men that made March successful. In short, the idea worked. Merten's employment was *so successful that it began to put* ideas in the minds of Galles and Mertens, who had separate ambitions of someday building their own chassis. Why take on the risk and financial burden of developing your own car while you 're winning races with a customer car? The answer came at the opening round of the 1992 season. Al Unser Jr., not exactly known for his qualifying savvy, put the new Galmer on the pole for its first race.

Previously, Galles had switched to Lola in 1989, and won the Championship with Lola in 1990. 1990 also saw the merger of Maurice Kraine's Kraco franchise to form Galles / Kraco Racing. Building one's own car was not a foreign idea to Kraines. In 1985, the Kraco team hired Don

raced. To this day, it remains a million dollar show car.

Galmer is located in the small but growing town of Bicester (pronounced bister). Housed in the former home of the once mighty March Engineering, Galmer is successfully taking on the big buck com-

I arrive in the lobby on Monday, February 3, 1992, red-eyed from lack of sleep and jet lag. Just as I announce myself and sit down, down the stairs comes Galles / Kraco mechanic Martin Fox. Fox looks at me as if I'm from outer space. This is the usual expression I receive from people who normally only see me at race tracks in North America. "Hi", he says confused. "I'm over here to do a piece on all of the race shops", I tell him. We chat for a couple of minutes then Martin gets back to work. Seconds later, down the stairs comes Paul 'Ziggy' Harcus who has been appointed chief mechanic for Danny Sullivan. Ziggy's entrance is a little more colorful: "What the f..., what are you doing here?" "I'm on a mission", I reply. "What, are you coming to work here?" "No, I'm doing a piece for my upcoming book" We talk briefly and then Ziggy heads through the door that leads to the assembly area.

I'm given a tour of the place and take some photos with the agreement

Former March boss, Robin Herd, came to Galmers rescue by renting the young company a portion of the former March factory.

Rick Amabile Photo

34

that I won't take any shots of the new gearbox design. Although fatigued, Mertens is friendly and still has his wit intact.

IICR: First of all, how did you get together With Rick Galles? Why was the decision made to develop your own cars?

Alan Mertens: Rick didn't come to me specifically to build a new car. Back in December 1988, March had gone public and I did feel that the attention really wasn't in the right place. Motor racing was becoming more commercially orientated. All of the ingredients that were there earlier which made the company successful weren't there anymore. I wanted to get out. I got released from my contract. After I had been with March for thirteen or fourteen years, I found myself out on the street thinking 'what do I do now?' I had known Ed Nathman and he was team manager of Galles at the time. Ed and I were good friends. They had just gotten Chevy engines and just signed Junior (Al Unser,Jr.). They were running March cars. Galles had asked March for factory technical support and March wasn't really prepared to give them any support. That just typified how

March's attitude had changed toward motor racing. During the course of a conversation with Ed, he told me the situation they were in with March. I was invited over to the race team in Albuquerque. I sat down and met Rick and Junior. We were discussing the situation and I told them that I had left March so Rick asked me if I'd like to come to work for him full time. I said "Ok, fine". So I started the relationship with Galles and we had a hugely successful year compared with the other March runners that year, and even the Lola runners in 1988. We finished second in the Championship. Unfortunately Ed left to go to Newman / Haas, but I was really comfortable with the team and particularly with Junior, so I decided to stay. At the end of the season, we realized what a huge gain we had made over the '88 season. We had independently developed the March to make it work. The gains that we made weren't passed on to the other March runners because we weren't doing it through the factory. The most logical progression from that was that Rick said 'Why don't we start our own development company". That way whatever car we buy, we could

Mertens has established a sound relationship with 1990 PPG Indy Car Champion, Al Unser, Jr.

further develop the production cars to beat the opposition. In the early days, we were very few in numbers and short in money. It was actually my idea to keep buying production cars and improving them. '89 turned out to be sort of a lackluster year, but we again proved our point in '90. All this time we were expanding our design and manufacturing shop back in England at Galmer. It was just a logical expansion from what we had done so far. We decided to produce our own car and make it as uncopyable as possible. With the Lola being sort of generic, we wanted to produce a completely different beast from what everybody else was running. Hopefully they will be uncopyable. The situation we were in with March and Lola was that, to a certain extent, we made changes to the car which were visible, so they were there for anybody else with the same chassis to copy and get more advantage without doing any development work. With a unique chassis, you can make improvements and hopefully get ahead of the game.

IICR: Was there any talk of building the car in Albuquerque rather than in England?

Mertens: We discussed it but I think that the logistics and finances excluding the exchange rate at that time, it was better to do it in England. By the time we had gotten around to doing our own car, we had established a very strong base in England with all the relevant personel to do it. What is popularly referred to as the cottage industry in England is actually much stronger and immediately supportive of something like a race car program. There's a whole industry that just feeds off the motor racing community. You have the right design and engineering people, the carbon people, machine shops and fabrication shops who are catered to your own particular needs.

IICR: So England is sort of like the Silicon Valley of motor racing.

Mertens: Yeah, pretty much. It's the same way in Formula One racing. Most of the F-1 teams are based

Art Flores Photo

in England.

IICR: Do lower labor costs in England play a factor factor at all?

Mertens: I don't know. I don't think that labor is that much cheaper in England. Basically, the cost of living is higher in England anyway. You do have considerable exchange rate factors. It just depends on the peaks and valleys of the overall economy. Sometimes you have to drive some hard bargains. It just depends when you build your cars whether you 're competing with anybody else who's in the same progress. You 've got a small company like ours trying to get things done for the bare minimum, and you might go to a supplier who also builds stuff for Williams or McLaren. (Formula One teams) Of course, it's typical for them to take their business first because they can afford to pay top rates, so you can tend to get shoved to the back of the line. Labor isn't a clear cut thing anymore. It's not an obvious advantage or disadvantage.

IICR: How did you end up in the same former building as March Engineering?

Mertens: We originally shared a shop with Parallel Motions who build a lot of exhaust systems for Indy cars. They gave us a big help in originally renting us space for a very low cost. But the problem was that Parallel Motions does work for Lola. Lola didn't really know the relationship we had together and were concerned about secrecy. Eight per-

The administative end of Galmer.

cent of Parallel's business was from Lola. Lola was under the misconception that we were partners in business. Lola felt that maybe Parallel would come to us and tell us what they were doing. So Lola gave Parallel an ultimatum saying that they didn't feel comfortable with the situation, and if we didn't move out, they'd take their business elsewhere. Realizing this would ruin Parallel's business, we had to find another place fairly quickly. Adrem Engineering, who does a lot of our machining, was leasing the old March factory. They couldn't afford to keep the whole unit themselves and they had a lot more space then they needed. So Robin Herd (March Engineering's principal founder), being an old buddy of mine came to the rescue. He still owns the premises. He let us and Adrem split the place down the middle. He did us another great favor by renting it to us at a price lower than it would normally be. Our shop is about 7,500 square feet.

IICR: When did the production of the first Galmer chassis begin?

Mertens: About a week after the last race of 1990.

IICR: How many engineers andother people do you have?

Mertens: We have an engineering staff of five. We peaked at about twenty people total, which includes the people who come over from Galles / Kraco who help assemble the cars. We have just enough people to get by with the job that we've taken on. Obviously, we don't have the kind of budget that

The relatively small drawing office sits above the administrative offices. The large drawing board on the right is for drafting body work in full scale.

Penske has where they have about 70 people and do 1000 hours of wind tunnel testing. We're trying to compete with about 20 people and 200 hours of wind tunnel testing per year. We wind tunnel test at Mire.

IICR: If you could break it down, how much is spent for the actual development of the car versus the actual material costs?

Mertens: It depends whether you're building one car like our prototype car or if you 're going to build four cars. Or whether, like Lola you build thirty cars. I depends how much you advertise the development costs over the number of cars you 're building. We originally estimated that to do a proper development program for an Indy car where you 've got all your bases covered, we would spend between 1,250,000 to 1,500,000 pounds ($2,250,000 to $2,700,000). In real terms, due to financial restraints, we actually were only able to spend 640,000 pounds ($1,152,000 at the $1.80 per pound exchange rate) on the development and build the first car. So if you took out the material cost to build one car which is prohibitive, the development cost is much higher than the materials.

IICR: When you go and wind tunnel test, do they charge you by the hour or day or week? Can you reveal how much it costs?

Mertens: It costs us about 2,500 pounds per day ($4,500) excluding the labor costs of the engineers and excluding anything that you're testing. That's assuming that you've already got a model and have already designed and built the pieces that you 're testing. (Authors note: Be-fore you go for your calculator, 200 hours of wind tunnel = 20 days total time x $4,500 per day = $90,000 alone in wind tunnel expense.) We figured out that the (1 / 3 scale) model cost 37,000 pounds ($66,600) to build. That's just one model without any installation for the test. We try to get in a ten hour shift when we do test.

IICR: Who does your composite work?

Mertens: Comtech (which was located about thirty yards from Galmer) did the prototype car, then they went bankrupt in December

These two chassis are in the body work fitting stages on the main shop floor.

1991. Advanced Composites did all of the other cars.

IICR: As a designer, do you often see yourself going out in the shop and getting your hands dirty in helping with the model making or the fabrication?

Mertens: I'm always doing that. I seem to be at the factory day and night. One minute I'm trying to run the business, trying to sort out the accounts, trying to keep everything going right with the cash flow situation. The next minute I'll be involved with the P R, the next minute I'll be trying to engineer the car. The next minute I'm at the race track trying to work with the drivers, the next minute I'm at the wind tunnel, and the next minute I'm actually physically on the shop floor helping put things together. It's very difficult at times to focus my attention. All this time I'm also concentrating on the particular design areas where my expertise comes to mind. That can sometimes be a problem with doing that and running the company. I have to try to spread the load as much as I can. The people I 've got are absolutely fantastic, but I could use more. We all end up doing everything, that's the only way we survive. The girl who does the accounts, when she's not doing that she's sweeping the floor, making tea, working on the telephone switchboard, doing the buying, sometimes even jumping in the van and chasing parts. That's the problem we have.

IICR: What are some of the things that you learned at March that you use in running Galmer?

Mertens: There's an awful lot of common sense and practicality involved. It's learning to balance both. There's a lot of people in this business that can get lost in pure theory. I think that March was a good place to go through your apprenticeship. You learned all about motor racing from the ground up. You learned the really simple fundamental things all the way through the complex, academic type things that make it work. They taught you to balance the two together. You don't get so simple that you ignore the science and you don't get too academic or scientific that you actually ignore the practicality of motor racing. In motor racing, to be really successful requires a balance of both.

IICR: How long were you in charge of the Indy car project at March?

Mertens: I was in charge on and off. We always shared the responsibility with somebody else. In motor racing, you get people who get labelled some kind of superstar designer. At the end of the day, you need a figurehead, but he still can't do it all. You still need all the smart guys to back you up. These days race cars are so difficult to design. You've got the mechanical side, the aerodynamic side, the electronics side, the gearbox side, the engine side. You tend to get somebody who gets named as being totally responsible for the concept and the overall design of the car. But you 're always delegating different areas to the people who you 've got working for you who've got the expertise in that particular area. I guess that I carried the label for being responsible for some of the March cars. I was never responsible for the aerodynamics. We had a separate aerodynamicist.

IICR: Do you find yourself having a lot more freedom now at Galmer to do things that you 've always wanted to do?

Mertens: I've got more freedom as far as I make the rules. But I've got a lot of strain in running the business, whereas before at March, I could concentrate one hundred percent on the engineering. All of the other aspects of running the company were always taken care of by somebody else. Now, I'm it. I could have a lot more engineering freedom but that will probably happen more in the future. Right now I have to carry all of the other responsibilities as well. At March, I didn't care about the money aspect, that was somebody else's worry. I didn't have to worry about the sales or the commercialability of the company, or any of the employee's personal problems. I didn't have to worry about wages, costing or whether the roof leaked or not, or whether this or that

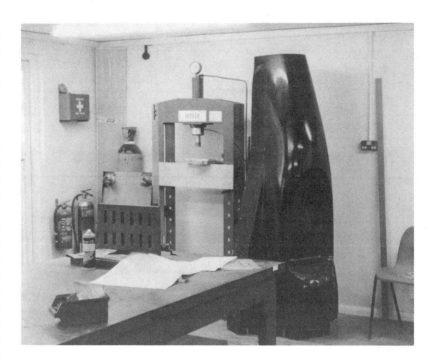

The full scale 'Buck' sits in the small composite room.

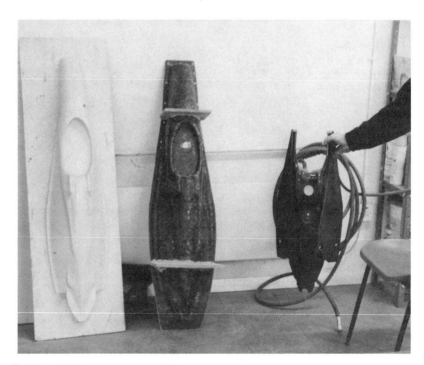

'Buck' and 'Molds' are also needed to produce the wind tunnel model. Here the 1/3 scale 'cowl' molds are shown.

gets done on time.

IICR: Is it pretty hard keeping everything secretive so that none of your technology leaks out to anybody else?

Mertens: I trust my people one hundred percent. They don't deliberately leak anything. But the thing is that when you take advantage of the industry in England, you become very visual. We use common foundries to do the tub so there's only certain people who've got the tub or the machining or whatever. We share wind tunnel facilities with other teams. So the suppliers we're dealing with try very hard to respect your confidentiallity, but you know that

38

your competitors can go in there and talk to them and maybe see a casting laying over in the corner, which they 're not shown, but they keep their eyes open. They may be able to see a drawing that's folded up on a bench where a guy is working, or they can see a certain piece laying around. Maybe a wind tunnel technician may say " Oh, that looks like so and so's car who was in here the other day". Nobody does it deliberately but it's so difficult to contain things with the enormous amount of people who come in contact with the project when it's designed and built.

IICR: Are there any plans in the future to make the Galmer chassis a production car if it becomes successsful?

Merterns: No, not a production car as such. It would be nice to try and alleviate the financial burden by selling some extra cars to produce the kind of money that Galmer needs to run properly. But we don't want it to become a strain on us as far as making sure that our primary concern is competitive. It would be nice if we could generate enough income to produce each new generation race car. In 1991, half way through the year all of our budget was used

up. We used it up just doing what was needed to be done and just covering our overhead.

IICR: Are you the overall idea man as far as the whole project, and as far as the shape of the car?

Mertens: No. I think what I do in all honesty is the same as what all of the other guys do, if this car was to be phenomenally sucessful, I haven't got a big ego and wouldn't say "yeah this is my car, I'm responsible for it". Because in reality it's not true and I don't think that it is true in any of the race car designs. I wouldn't say that it's designed by a committee, because that implies that there is no control over it. It's actually designed by a group of people. Not only do we do it democratically by arguing through ideas back at the factory, but also there's a huge input from the team. From the drivers and mechanics. I suppose one person has to ultimately be the arbitrator by trying to pull all of the information together and turn it around in to something that's cohesive.

IICR: How do you and the guys discuss new ideas? Do you just bounce things off each other?

Mertens: Yeah, and they come from anywhere. They might come from

Danny (Sullivan) or from Junior, or they may come from Owen (Snyder, Al Jr.'s chief mechanic) or (Team manager) Barry Green, or any of the engineers who might of come up with something that they 've seen in a picture or a pure brainstorm. We'll sit down, we'll all talk it through, we'll argue it, we'll look at all of the pros and cons. We'll see how integrated it is with the rest of the program that we're trying to achieve. We go along like that. I think in reality everyone does that.

IICR: Are there ever instances where you or one of the design team might be driving to work and all of the sudden you think of a new idea and go in to work and say " I've got this great idea"?

Mertens: Oh yeah, all the time. If fact, you couldn't have used a better analogy. Sometimes when the day's over and done with, you get in the car and you sit down and relax, you 're thinking that you 're relaxing. You 're not consciously trying to weave your way through all of the pros and cons of a design. You 're trying to relax and all of the sudden an idea just surfaces. It could be when you are going home or coming to work, or sometimes when you' re laying in bed at night and you 're trying to forget about your work and trying to get to sleep, something just comes to you. You have to try and hold on to it. It's something that doesn't leave you alone. You have to write it down, get it on a piece of paper before you can get to sleep. Sometimes you can wake up early in the morning waiting for the alarm to go off and something hits you then. There's no hard rules whether you're a scientist or an aircraft designer or whatever. That's typical in a lot of areas.

Amabile: Yeah, I get a lot of ideas the same way.

IICR: What kind of computer system do you use in design?

Mertens: It's a CAD. We would like something that could do solid modeling and surface work, but they cost a lot of money. But the CAD is wonderful for what we us it for. It's ex-

Much of Galmers machine pieces are produced by next door neighbor ADREM Engineering.

tremely efficient. It's extremely good value for the money.

IICR: How much does a system like that cost?

Mertens: In England, the retail price for a system like that, for the hardware and software, costs around 8-10,000 pounds ($14,400 -$18,000) per station. We only have one station and the guys love it, they 're always fighting over it! The programs we use are designed for the general engineering field.

IICR: We've all seen the car cutaways that Tony Matthews draws for various manufacturers. Do you ever look at those and learn anything from your competition?

Mertens: Oh, sure. (laughing)

IICR: If you learn that much, why does each manufacturer release them?

Mertens: Generally speaking, you have to accept that all of your competitors are really switched on, they walk around with their eyes open. After the first two races of each year, the cars go through tech, they see

them being worked on under the awning. They've pretty much seen what there is to bloody see anyway. If you're lucky enough to get a cutaway drawing early enough it might be useful to you, but you never do. All of the design cycles are the same. It could be a memory jogger for the following year. You think "that's a good idea, maybe we should think about that". It's just like a very good photograph. Tony has been commissioned by Valvoline to do our car also, it was released in time for Long Beach.

IICR: How many years behind Formula One do you estimate Indycars are as far as technology?

Mertens: That's a very difficult question to answer. In some respects, you talk about active suspension (where sensors aboard the car adjust to bumps and send a signal to hydraulic rams to automatically adjust the cars ride height within a split second) and semi-automatic gear boxes (where the driver selects the gears by pressing buttons

mounted on the back of the steering wheel) and stuff like that, then we're probably five or six years behind. But that's not because the people involved in Indy car racing aren't capable of doing it, it's because the regulations strictly prohibit it.

IICR: What about aerodynamics?

Mertens: I think Lola has set the standard for that in the last two years. I think their 1990 and 1991 cars drew a lot of experience and ideas from their Formula One program. They turned it around. All of the sudden, you see the Penske and TrueSports cars and our cars have actually followed in those leads. The others might be too proud to admit it, but you only have to look at the cars and you can see it. We're following in Lola's lead and taking a more keener interest in Formula One aerodynamics and actually applying that to an Indy car. Aerodynamically, Indy cars are catching up quite quickly. I don't think, other than those two examples, that Indy cars are far behind. I think they 're just

Al Unser, Jr. and Danny Sullivan will use the Galmer chassis to try to overcome Little Al's disappointing late race crash that cost him a 1989 Indianapolis 500 win.

Steve Weaver Photo

different. They do a different job and the regulations are different.

IICR: Are there ever any small things that you guys come up with that's never been tried in F-1 that they could maybe use?

Mertens: Sure, a lot of things because they don't run on ovals. The Formula One guys sometimes come over to our shop and they see what we do to our cars to make them run on ovals, and they think it's hilarious. But then they sit down and think about it and they can see the logic behind it. There's a lot of little neat tricks that you do which help on ovals. There's a lot of little neat tricks that they do which help them on road courses which they design in to the car. We can't design those things into our cars because if we did, we wouldn't be able to run it on an oval. All of their business with monoshocks (where there is just a single spring / damper unit in front) you can't really do that and run on ovals. Some of the things that we do on our more conventional suspension cars, they wouldn't dream of doing on their cars because they don't run on ovals. From the lay men's point of view, if you look at a car that is set up for an oval with tilt, stager, positive camber on one wheel and negative camber on the other side, it looks like it's already had an accident!

IICR: When you start out to design a car, what comes first?

Mertens: The first thing we do is a one third scale complete drawing of the total package of the car. From that you build a wind tunnel model to test the aerodynamics, that comes first. From there on in after you 've already been to the wind tunnel, you try and get a balance of the aerodynamic and mechanical side as they compliment each other. You compromise the two, but always the aerodynamics come first.

IICR: You have a real good working relationship with Al Unser, Jr. What impresses you the most about little Al?

Mertens: His feel for the car, his eloquence in the way he puts it (how the car feels) across. His attention to detail. He refuses to go around a problem, he refuses to get caught up in what we call "chasing

You will notice the small GALMER logo near the number 5 on the side of the car. In 1992 that name was now on the serial number plate in the cockpit.

Steve Weaver Photo

the clock". He won't go out there and drive the shit out of the car just for the sake of driving the shit out of the car just to post a good time. He doesn't just keep driving around. He goes out and runs fast enough to feel the car, then he comes in and tells us the changes that are needed to have a better race car. That's the way he goes about it. More often than not, that always means that you 've got a very good driveable race car. Racing is much more important to him than pole positions or sitting on the front row of the grid. It's that approach that also helps us in

the development of the car. The other thing is that we get along so well with each other. That means that we can talk to each other in a way that might make us uncomfortable or embarrassed if we were talking to someone else. If I make a mistake, I don't feel uncomfortable admitting it to him because I know he won't think " you stupid ass, what the hell did you do that for". We say "okay fine, get on with it". We can have arguments, we can be really shouting and screaming at each other one minute, then the next minute after we 've gotten the problem sorted out, it doesn't even leave a bitter taste in his mouth. We're such good buddies that we don't have to try and forget it, it just comes naturally. With this rapport that we've developed between us, we 'll do and discuss whatever it takes, however bizarre it may seem, however off the wall or however embarrassing it is. It's so honest and open. That's a huge asset to the team.

IICR: As far as the motor racing industry as a whole, how much would you say the average engineer makes per year?

Mertens: I'd say that a draftsman makes around 20,000 pounds up to a senior engineer at about 35-40,000 pounds. A senior engineer-designer-race engineer, who has to travel a lot, between 50-80,000 pound per year. Formula One designers, I hear stories of 100-150-200,000 pounds per year. At Galmer, our wage structure does run, from the engineering point of view, from 20-55,000 pounds. Assemblers can earn, because they are on an hourly scale and earn overtime pay, they can earn from 20-30,000, without busting their asses and seeing their wives and children.

IICR: How do you cope with working so hard and traveling so much? You probably have to hop the pond every few weeks, right?

Mertens: Yeah, you learn to live with it. I think that it's probably far worse on my family than it is on me. My wife is proud of what I do and she enjoys the money that we can make. It's not a huge amount of money, but we're not poor. But she says she doesn't want the money, she wants a husband and a father first. It's harder on her. She misses me, she misses my company. My children particularly, I hope that they don't suffer. One's three and the other seven years old. They like their daddy to be around as well. Daddy , when there's not too much pressure at work, can be good fun. I can see it in their little faces when I go home, I can see how much I'm missed. It's a lot harder on my family.

IICR: How many trips back and forth per year do you usually make? Do you have an apartment in the States?

Mertens: In 1991, because I was so involved in the new car I only made eight trips. In a typical year, when I do support the team throughout the whole season of testing and racing, about 17 or 18 trips. I just stay at hotels. I don't spend much time in Albuquerque, I just spend my time wherever we're at on the racing schedule.

IICR: Do you still talk to Robin Herd very often?

Mertens: Not very often now. Of course we're leasing the shop from him. He's now involved with the Larrousse Formula One team. We do have a close relationship. I remember when he came back from a Laguna(Seca) test. He said "Alan, I never, ever believed that what you were setting up to achieve would be sucessful". He said, "I'm amazed". After you left March I had conversations with people who said that Alan was stupid, he's never going to make it work". He said that he's pleased

that it actually did. He said he's pleased for me and he was going to unashamedly copy it! He did, he went ahead and did the same sort of design concept for his F-1 car. He calls it "The other Galmer"! We took on a lot to develop our own car. Galmer and Galles / Kraco, we're good at this. We're good fighters. There's a lot of good people here. I get a huge amount of support. We'll get it done.

A word about pay in the U.K.

Over the course of my experience in Indy car racing, I was always told by mechanics, who were formally employed by British teams, that pay in the U. K. was low. This seemed to make since because a lot of these mechanics, usually from Formula 1 racing, had packed up their tool boxes and headed to the United States. Overall, I'm told that the pay is relatively low in England. Is it really that low in the motor racing industry, it all depends on who you talk to. Paul Morgan of Ilmor Engineering said earlier in the book that pay in England and in most of Europe for that matter is lower than that of the United States. Other sources, like Alan Mertens of Galmer and Mike Blanchet of Lola have indicated that the salary scale in Britain's motor racing industry has reached higher levels in recent years. I was thinking about this subject while I was walking down the street in Northampton. I came across an employment agency and decided to stop and look at the jobs that were advertised in the window, and studied how much each job paid. Being the curious individual that I am, I walked into the agency to do some investigating. After explaining my curiosity, I was able to ask an agent just how the British public faired in the salary catagory. I came to find out that it's not much after all compared to pay in the United States, but then again, I was inquiring about the incomes of normal people in normal jobs. All figures are in Pounds.

Police and Fireman: About 15-17,000 .
Doctors: (Britain has Socialized medicine) 35-50,000.
Machinists in normal industry:

15 - 18,000
Autoworkers:
15 - 18,000
Secretarys:
10,000
Accountants:
25,000
Waiter and Bartenders:
2.50 - 3.00 per hour, plus tips.

These figures seem at first to be somewhat relative with jobs in America only if you consider the 1.8 exchange rate. However, let's consider the cost of living in England. A two-bedroom, one-bathroom apartment in Northampton rents for about 300 pounds per month. I get a laugh when I inquire how much extra for two bathrooms because they are very uncommon. The average power and gas bill is 75 pounds per month. As you can see, the cost of living is not scaled down to the 1.8 exchange rate. So how much are good and services ? They too are also not scaled down. Lets say that you go to McDonalds in England and order a Big Mac. It would cost around 1.75 Pounds. In America, they cost around $1.75. Lets say you need to buy a television. In America, a T.V. might cost around $400 - 500. The same T.V. would cost 400-500 Pounds. From these examples, you can see that the cost of living is a little tighter in England. Having socialized medicine is one advantage, but it costs nine percent of your wage. Even more costly are the taxes. The income tax is 25 % up to 23,000 Pounds. It rises to 40 % above that. No wonder Nigel Mansell moved to Florida!

The drive through menu at a Mc Donald's restaurant in North London

Rick Amabile

Penske Cars

I n the mid 1970's, Roger Penske decided to go Formula 1 racing. The next step was to establish a snop in the U.K. that wasn't far from the European circuit. Although the Formula 1 project was short lived, the shop and staff still remained. Today, Penske Cars remains as the constructors of the most expensive cars in Indy car racing. Each Penske chassis is estimated to cost at least twice as much as a Lola. Why is this? Let's look at the numbers involved. Roger Penske's U. K. operation employs a total of 70 people, about 65 percent of the force employed by Lola. Yet Penske only builds around 25 percent of the cars that Lola ships out. Although no exact figure is ever released, it is pretty safe to estimate that each car Penske builds has a price tag that soars into the upper six figure range. Big money. Penske's English payroll alone could cover the cost of six Lola chassis. The fruits of all of this time and expense is that Roger Penske reigns as probably the biggest name in Indy car racing. Penske Cars Ltd. delivers the results.

On my arrival to Poole, I discovered that the town is actually bigger than I thought. I'm told by a taxi driver that around 130,000 people call Poole home. To my surprise, the driver actually has some general clues to where the mighty Penske's English shop is located. We drive through the Upton Industrial Estate and find the brick building rather easily.

Poole is located along the English channel. Penske's 17,500 square foot shop is managed by Nick Goozee. Nick joined the Penske camp in 1974 as a fabricator. Previously, he was employed by the

Although you probably wouldn't notice it by driving by, this is the building where five Indy winning chassis have been built.

Brabham Formula 1 team dating back to 1963. Goozee moved up the ladder becoming general manager in 1983, director in 1985 and finally managing director in 1990. Since the mid 70's, Penske Cars has constructed 76 cars ranging from the PC-01 to the current Penske Chevy '92.

A list of Penske's all time victories adorns the small reception area.

IICR: Tell me a little bit why Penske Racing chooses to build its race cars in England rather than in America? Is it because off all of the resources close by ?

Nick Goozee: Yes, the United Kingdom is the world's center of Motor Sport. With few exceptions the majority of the leading race car manufacturers are based here, or have satellite companies based here. Perhaps more significantly, the expertise and craftsmanship required to design and build competition cars are readily available. Geographically all suppli

ers and specialized sub-contractors are easily accessible, being within a maximum radius of 300 miles. In the United States or Europe, these distances can be many times greater.

IICR: How many people are on the payroll in England alone? Can you break down how many in each area?

Goozee: We currently have about 70 people at Penske Cars:

- 10 Fabricators
- 4 Pattern shop
- 8 Machinists
- 18 Composites
- 2 Inspectors

Rick Amabile Photo

9 Design / Engineering
4 Model makers
8 Administration
4 Maintenance

IICR: Why do you do your own composite work rather than sub-contracting the work? Can you reveal what your annual composite budget?

Goozee : Composites are very expensive. We can expect to pay upwards of $60 an hour to have com

In typical fashion, the drawing office is always kept busy.

posites made outside, and that's without any guarantees of quality or having them delivered on time. In order for us to have total control of both, together with considerably reduced costs in the long run, it is essential to have our own composite shop in-house. Confidentiality is also a bonus. We spend in excess of $500,000 per year on composites.

IICR: As technology progresses, is the composite process getting any less expensive?

Goozee: No, not really. Technology always has and always will cost money. The more advanced we get, the more it costs.

IICR: Why Poole? Would it be easier to base near London?

Goozee : No, it's actually better that we're in this part on the country. Poole is only 1 hour 20 minutes drive from Heathrow. We have an advantage when our labor force is 'out of reach from all the other teams based around London, and there

fore we are able to retain staff for long periods. We also enjoy a level of exclusivity amongst our local suppliers and sub-contractors, which can often work very much to our advantage.

IICR: When do you start the development process of each car? Can you tell me about how many design hours it takes for each new design?

Goozee : Generally, the develop

ment of a new chassis starts almost immediately after Indianapolis. We generally expect a total elapsed time of five to six months, depending upon how many changes there are over the previous chassis. Serious detail designs start to appear during

September and we aim to have the prototype finished during January. It's difficult to estimate the exact design time. A rough guess would be between 10-12,000 hours.

IICR: How many assembly hours go in to each new chassis? Where do you start?

Goozee : We always make a mock-up first. This comprises a complete chassis. We take the new bodywork made from the new molds and put them together with the underwing, side pods and a see through engine cover. This allows for all of the body assembly work to be done away from the first real car. There's nothing worse than having to try and fit bodywork on to a car while it is being assembled, and vice versa. 'Real car' assembly takes 2-3 weeks. We only actually assemble one complete car in Poole. The remainder of the cars are shipped to the shop in Reading (PA) in the form of kits. Each kit takes four full weeks to build all of the pieces.

IICR: Who are the other engineers under Nigel Bennett?

Goozee : Principally there is Geoff Ferris. He was the chief designer of all Penske cars from the PC-01 to the PC-12. He is now in charge of designing our transmissions.

IICR: I was going to ask you what ever happened to him? Do you see any benefits in designing cars for two specific drivers like Rick Mears

Similar to other manufacturers, CAD/CAM technology is used quite extensively in the design stages.

and Emerson Fittipaldi? I mean, Rick is 5' 10" and Emmo is 5' 8".

Goozee : Perhaps it is a little easier. With a few exceptions most drivers will fit most cars.

IICR: Why hasn't Penske made the move to get into producing cars for customers like you were doing in the late 1970's and early 80's? Wouldn't that be a lot more cost effective?

Goozee : We have invested a huge amount of time and effort to try to be the best, and exclusive. If we ever have any advantages then our drivers must be allowed to enjoy them. I must say that it is also embarrassing to be beaten by one of our own cars, which of course is what happened to us in 1989 when we sold cars to Patrick Racing and were beaten at Indy. We are not really geared for mass production anyway. I think that very few teams would be prepared to pay double the price for one of our cars as opposed to buying a Lola.

IICR: When Penske allows a certain budget for each year, is it hard to keep within that budget in areas such as wind tunnel expense?

Goozee : Wind tunnel expenses are easy to budget as we have a contractual agreement that stipulates the amount for each year. Costs beyond that are fairly easy to predict. Our budget is set for a fixed number of cars, spares, hours and expenses. If we keep to the expected figures then we are within budget, but motor racing is full of the unexpected and that has to be paid for. Experience helps!

IICR: How many hours of wind tunnel time go into each car? How much does this time cost?

Goozee : We spend 18 (6 day) weeks in the wind tunnel each year. In 1993, we will sign a new contract that will raise this to 22 weeeks from '93 onwards. When we test, we run an average of 10 hours per day, so around 1,080 hours of wind tunnel testing per year. The daily rate varies between customers, but it does represent a large portion of our budget.

IICR: As far as suspension design

A full size 'Buck' is made as a pattern to 'lay up' composite materials into the various body pieces. The Buck is made from mostly wood and clay.

In typical Penske tradition, the shop floor is kept spotless. The autoclave is in the rear of the photo.

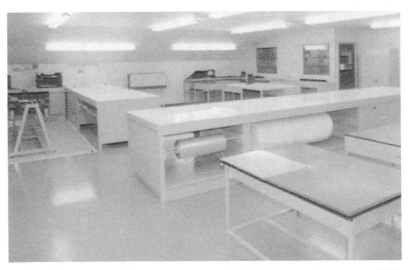

You will notice the rolls of Carbon fiber beneath a bench in the composite room. This room is cleaned to resemble this photo at the end of each day.

goes, is there any sort of simulator that you use to test rather than strictly track time?

Goozee : I expect that there is, but we do not use one. We can simulate all of our suspension and its reaction on our Computervision C.A.D. system. This is extremely accurate and saves large quantities of time, but at the end of the day there is no substitute to rubber on the track, because no simulator can equate with continually changing track conditions.

IICR: How do you account for so many people building only 6 or 7 cars per year when you only had maybe 8 or 10 employees doing it in the 1970's?

Goozee : In the 70's, and 60's cars were very simple. In fact a Formula 1 or Indy car of those days was no more complicated than a small formula car is nowadays. When I started at Penske two of us did all of the fabrication and only 6 people went to a Grand Prix! At Brabham (Formula 1 team) two of us made every part of each car and that included the chassis. I was there from 1968 to 1973. Of course, nowadays the cars

Four time Indy winner Rick Mears is usually the first to 'shake down' each new design. If Rick comes in after an initial test and replies, "we've got ourselves a race car", you know that the competition is in trouble !

Nick Goozee poses with the first Penske-Chevy '92.

are highly complex. To really produce them in a sensible time frame requires a large number of people. Also, back in the 70's the team only had two cars total, now it's five or six. These require many spares and many alternatives. In the 70's you raced with what you started with, and that was it. Period! □

Steve Weaver Photo

1989 Championship winner Emerson Fittipaldi does his stuff at Detroit in 1990.

The United Kingdom

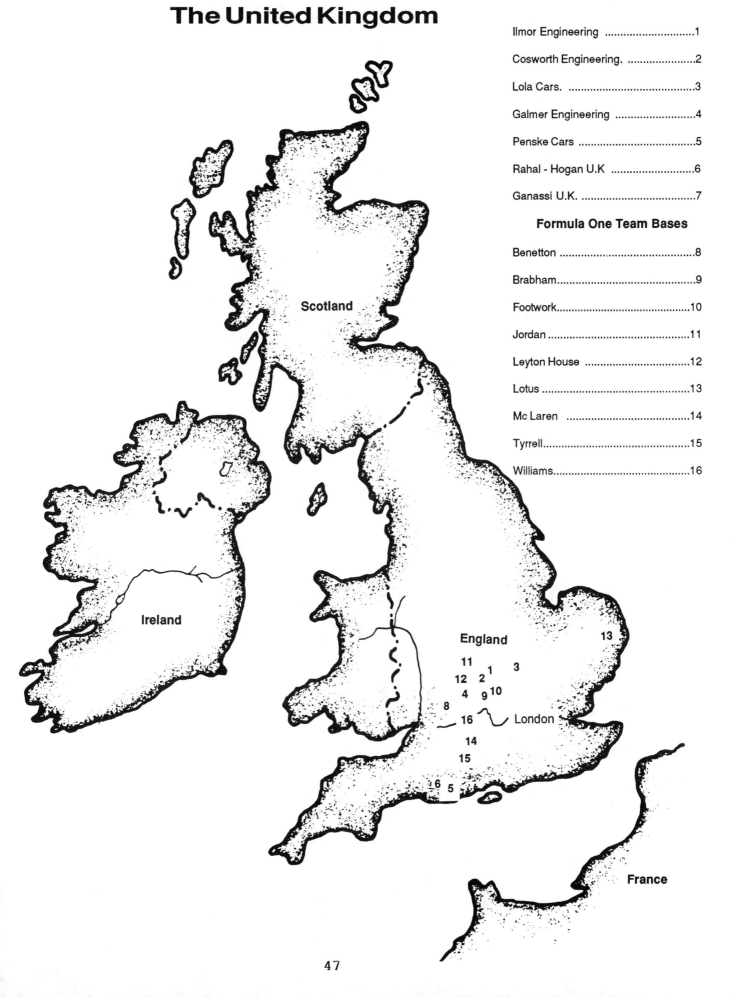

England Shop Locations

Ilmor Engineering	1
Cosworth Engineering.	2
Lola Cars.	3
Galmer Engineering	4
Penske Cars	5
Rahal - Hogan U.K	6
Ganassi U.K.	7

Formula One Team Bases

Benetton	8
Brabham	9
Footwork	10
Jordan	11
Leyton House	12
Lotus	13
Mc Laren	14
Tyrrell	15
Williams	16

Scotland

Ireland

England

London

France

The Law of Averages

Michael Andretti has one of the most impressive average patterns, rising steadily up over his career.

Who's currently the best Indy car driver? Who's the best qualifier? Who's the best finisher? These questions have always been asked by race fans and the media alike. Just who is the best Indy car driver as far as ability? Is Rick Mears a better driver than A.J. Foyt? Is Michael Andretti a better driver than Little Al? The world will never know. However, what can we judge? The answer is statistics. Can statistics tell us who is the best driver as far as ability, probably not. Factors such as the quality of equipment that a drivers has dealt with over the years make any true judgments hard to justify. Some drivers have had good equipment for most of their careers, while others have not.

These statistics are presented in graph form, not to gauge who's good and who's bad, but rather to take an interesting look at who is doing what. As you will see, all drivers have their peaks and pitfalls. These drivers all have good years and bad years. You can see this over the next ten pages. The results of this study can be a great acknowledgement for some drivers. Others will view this as a source of embarrassment. The results are not presented in any special order until we come to 'The Judgment Page'. Here, you can see the final results of this research. All numbers represent starts in various sized fields, both oval and road course events. This is to get an overall reading, without the need for separate graphs for larger and smaller fields of competitors.

All graphs are presented with the drivers average start in broken lines. The average finish is chronicaled in solid lines.

It's judgment day. Let's see who has performed well and who hasn't over the last 13 years.

Starting Average

■ ■ ■ ■ ■ ■ ■ ■ ■

Finishing Average

———————

48

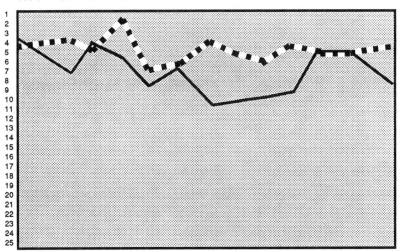

	1979	80	81	82	83	84	85	86	87	88	89	90	91
AVERAGE START	4.46	3.75	5.64	1.67	7.61	7.18	4.40	6.82	7.80	3.20	3.73	3.75	3.47
AVERAGE FINISH	3.07	7.17	4.82	6.00	9.62	7.27	11.4	11.65	10.4	9.00	5.27	5.38	7.94
NUMBER OF STARTS	14	12	11	12	13	11	5	17	15	15	15	16	17
CHAMPION-SHIP FINISH	1st	4th	1st	1st	6th	5th	10th	8th	5th	4th	2nd	3rd	4th

'90 Marlboro Challenge Winner
Rick Mears

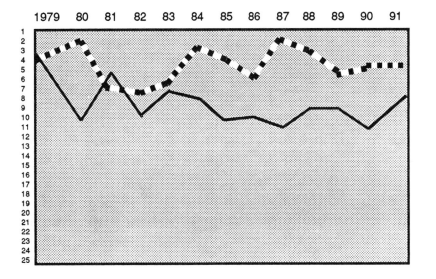

	1979	80	81	82	83	84	85	86	87	88	89	90	91
AVERAGE START	4.00	1.75	7.00	7.67	6.31	2.44	4.64	5.94	2.47	3.20	5.67	5.19	5.12
AVERAGE FINISH	3.00	10.00	5.38	9.67	7.62	8.75	10.43	10.18	11.00	9.40	9.67	10.31	7.71
NUMBER OF STARTS	1	4	8	12	13	16	14	17	15	15	15	16	17
CHAMPION-SHIP FINISH	11th	16th	11th	3rd	3rd	1st	5th	5th	6th	5th	6th	7th	7th

Mario Andretti

A.J. Foyt

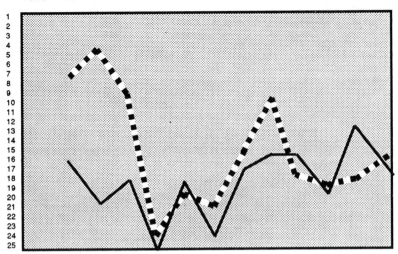

	1979	80	81	82	83	84	85	86	87	88	89	90	91
AVERAGE START		7.00	4.50	9.17	24.00	19.8	21.5	15.25	9.33	17.00	19.50	18.00	16.63
AVERAGE FINISH		16.50	19.50	17.67	31.00	19.80	23.67	16.75	15.00	15.57	19.50	12.86	18.63
NUMBER OF STARTS	NO STARTS IN CART SERIES	2	2	6	1	5	6	8	14	14	12	14	8
CHAMPION-SHIP FINISH		44th	49th	28th	37th	31st	41st	21st	23rd	16th	18th	11th	30th

Tony Bettenhausen

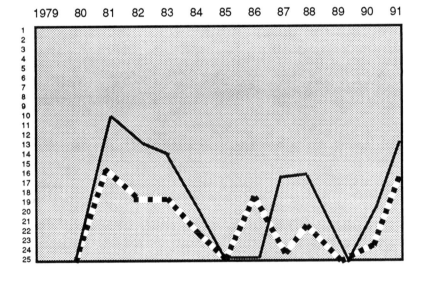

	1979	80	81	82	83	84	85	86	87	88	89	90	91
AVERAGE START		31.00	15.50	17.91	17.54	22.50	29.00	18.00	24.22	21.08	26.00	23.45	16.88
AVERAGE FINISH		32.00	10.10	12.64	13.77	19.75	29.00	28.00	15.78	15.67	26.00	18.91	12.94
NUMBER OF STARTS	NO STARTS IN CART SERIES	1	10	11	13	4	1	1	9	12	1	11	17
CHAMPION-SHIP FINISH		63rd	6th	10th	17th	40th	41st	36th	29th	17th	50th	24th	14th

Scott Brayton

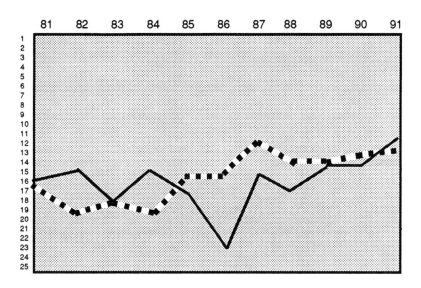

	1981	82	83	84	85	86	87	88	89	90	91
AVERAGE START	16.73	19.60	18.17	19.38	15.50	15.60	12.80	14.25	14.07	13.67	12.94
AVERAGE FINISH	15.82	14.60	18.76	14.62	17.70	22.60	14.80	17.25	14.21	13.94	11.82
NUMBER OF STARTS	11	5	6	13	10	5	5	12	14	16	17
CHAMPION- SHIP FINISH	13th	33rd	24th	23rd	22nd	36th	22nd	23rd	15th	15th	12th

'89 Michigan 500 Winner
Michael Andretti

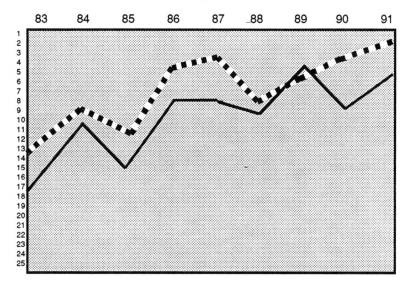

	1983	84	85	86	87	88	89	90	91
AVERAGE START	13.00	8.25	11.53	4.35	3.60	7.53	6.13	3.88	2.35
AVERAGE FINISH	17.33	10.31	14.93	7.65	7.87	9.00	5.33	8.06	5.82
NUMBER OF STARTS	3	16	15	17	15	15	15	16	17
CHAMPION- SHIP FINISH	26th	7th	9th	2nd	2nd	6th	3rd	2nd	1st

51

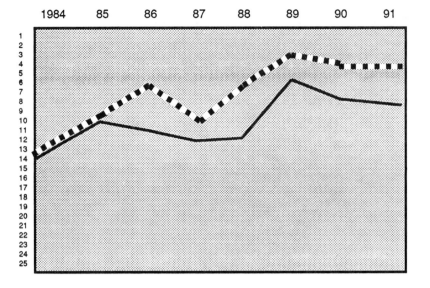

'90 Indy Qualifying Record Holder
Emerson Fittipaldi

	1984	85	86	87	88	89	90	91
AVERAGE START	13.44	9.53	6.65	10.27	6.53	3.33	4.31	4.12
AVERAGE FINISH	13.56	10.13	11.35	11.93	11.20	5.33	7.50	8.82
NUMBER OF STARTS	9	15	17	15	15	15	16	17
CHAMPION- SHIP FINISH	15th	6th	7th	10th	7th	1st	5th	5th

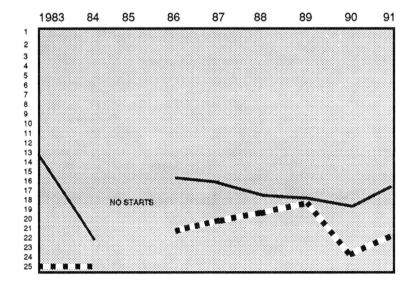

Randy Lewis

	1983	84	85	86	87	88	89	90	91
AVERAGE START	27.00	25.00	NO STARTS	21.25	20.71	19.43	18.43	23.19	22.45
AVERAGE FINISH	13.00	15.25	--	15.25	16.71	17.14	17.80	18.44	16.73
NUMBER OF STARTS	1	3	--	8	14	14	14	16	11
CHAMPION- SHIP FINISH	37th	40th	--	24th	21st	29th	35th	28th	29th

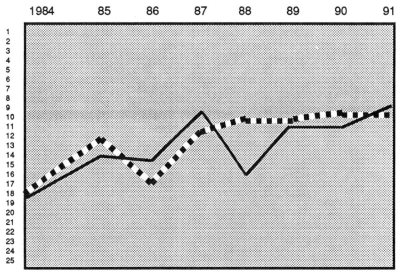

	1984	85	86	87	88	89	90	91
AVERAGE START	18.00	12.33	17.47	11.40	10.07	9.93	9.19	9.82
AVERAGE FINISH	8.00	14.17	14.33	8.80	16.47	10.87	10.81	9.00
NUMBER OF STARTS	1	12	15	15	15	15	16	17
CHAMPION-SHIP FINISH	34th	18th	17th	7th	14th	10th	8th	6th

Arie Luyendyk

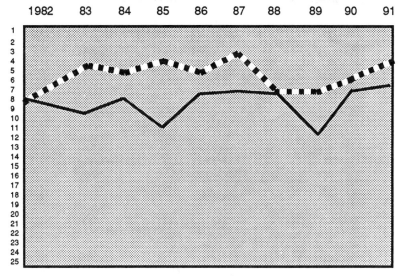

	1982	83	84	85	86	87	88	89	90	91
AVERAGE START	8.00	3.92	5.13	4.13	5.24	3.53	6.93	7.33	5.60	4.24
AVERAGE FINISH	7.73	9.00	7.63	11.40	7.29	7.07	7.33	12.13	7.25	6.29
NUMBER OF STARTS	11	12	16	15	17	15	15	15	16	17
CHAMPION-SHIP FINISH	2nd	5th	3rd	3rd	1st	1st	3rd	9th	4th	2nd

Bobby Rahal

53

'89 Pocono 500 Winner
Danny Sullivan

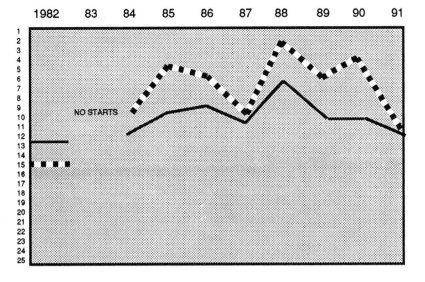

	1982	83	84	85	86	87	88	89	90	91
AVERAGE START	14.00	NO STARTS	9.19	4.73	6.18	8.93	2.40	6.15	3.44	10.71
AVERAGE FINISH	12.67		11.94	9.27	8.65	10.60	7.07	10.08	10.06	12.00
NUMBER OF STARTS	3	--	16	15	17	15	15	13	16	17
CHAMPION-SHIP FINISH	22nd	--	4th	4th	3rd	9th	1st	7th	6th	11th

Al Unser, Jr.

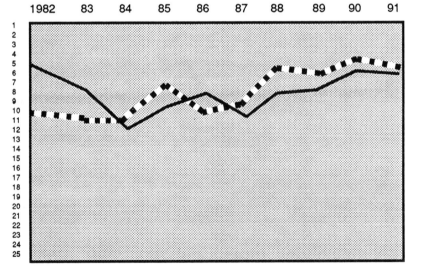

	1982	83	84	85	86	87	88	89	90	91
AVERAGE START	10.00	10.46	10.63	7.13	10.00	9.27	5.07	6.13	4.69	5.24
AVERAGE FINISH	5.00	7.92	12.25	8.93	7.88	10.33	8.13	7.87	5.88	6.06
NUMBER OF STARTS	1	13	16	15	17	15	15	15	16	17
CHAMPION-SHIP FINISH	21st	7th	6th	2nd	4th	3rd	2nd	5th	1st	3rd

John Andretti

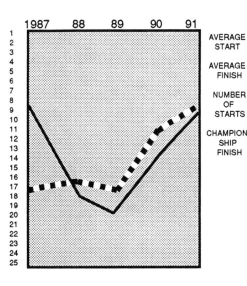

	1987	88	89	90	91
AVERAGE START	17.20	16.00	17.50	11.50	8.64
AVERAGE FINISH	8.60	18.09	20.33	13.38	9.59
NUMBER OF STARTS	5	11	6	16	17
CHAMPION-SHIP FINISH	17th	31st	33rd	10th	8th

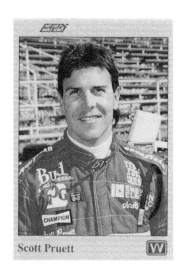

Scott Pruett

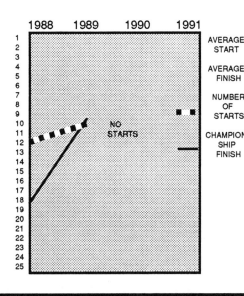

	1988	1989	1990	1991
AVERAGE START	12.33	10.40	NO STARTS	8.47
AVERAGE FINISH	18.00	9.20		12.00
NUMBER OF STARTS	3	15	--	17
CHAMPION-SHIP FINISH	38th	8th	--	10th

John Jones

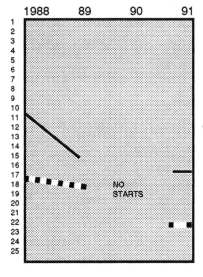

	1988	89	90	91
AVERAGE START	17.21	18.71	NO STARTS	22.10
AVERAGE FINISH	10.64	15.21		16.00
NUMBER OF STARTS	11	14	--	10
CHAMPION-SHIP FINISH	11th	17th	--	18th

55

Didier Theys

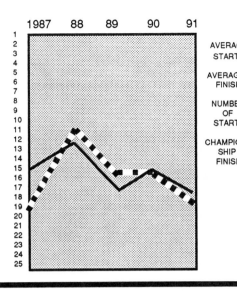

	1987	88	89	90	91
AVERAGE START	19.33	10.75	15.67	15.58	19.89
AVERAGE FINISH	15.33	12.75	17.25	15.75	18.00
NUMBER OF STARTS	3	8	12	12	9
CHAMPIONSHIP FINISH	30th	15th	21st	18th	25th

Scott Goodyear

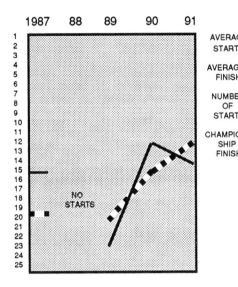

	1987	88	89	90	91
AVERAGE START	19.43	NO STARTS	20.00	15.13	12.12
AVERAGE FINISH	15.57		23.00	12.75	14.00
NUMBER OF STARTS	7	--	2	16	17
CHAMPIONSHIP FINISH	28th	--	48th	13th	13th

Mike Groff

	1990	91
AVERAGE START	17.00	14.31
AVERAGE FINISH	15.00	14.92
NUMBER OF STARTS	12	13
CHAMPIONSHIP FINISH	17th	16th

Hiro Matsushita

	1990	91
AVERAGE START	23.20	18.76
AVERAGE FINISH	18.30	14.71
NUMBER OF STARTS	10	17
CHAMPIONSHIP FINISH	31st	21st

	1986	90	91
AVERAGE START	11.00	11.94	9.94
AVERAGE FINISH	27.00	10.5	9.71
NUMBER OF STARTS	1	16	17
CHAMPION-SHIP FINISH	36th	9th	9th

Eddie Cheever

	1991
AVERAGE START	11.50
AVERAGE FINISH	18.75
NUMBER OF STARTS	4
CHAMPION-SHIP FINISH	21st

Paul Tracy

	1990	91
AVERAGE START	18.00	18.44
AVERAGE FINISH	20.75	15.67
NUMBER OF STARTS	8	9
CHAMPION-SHIP FINISH		26th	17th

Willy T. Ribbs

	1990	91
AVERAGE START	16.00	15.65
AVERAGE FINISH	17.00	13.35
NUMBER OF STARTS	1	17
CHAMPION-SHIP FINISH	39th	15th

Jeff Andretti

	1990	91
AVERAGE START	22.83	20.60
AVERAGE FINISH	18.67	21.10
NUMBER OF STARTS	6	10
CHAMPION-SHIP FINISH	30th	21st

Buddy Lazier

	1991
AVERAGE START	16.75
AVERAGE FINISH	18.25
NUMBER OF STARTS	12
CHAMPION-SHIP FINISH	19th

Ted Prappas

The Judgment Page

Combined Starting Averages from 1979 - 1991

1	Mario Andretti	4.72
2	Rick Mears	4.88
3	Bobby Rahal	5.41
4	Michael Andretti	6.74
5	Emerson Fittipaldi	7.27
6	Danny Sullivan	7.30
7	Al Unser Jr.	7.86
8	Scott Pruett	10.40
9	Eddie Cheever	10.96
10	Paul Tracy	11.50
11	Arie Luyendyk	12.28
12	John Andretti	14.17
13	A.J. Foyt Jr.	15.14
14	Mike Groff	15.66
15	Scott Brayton	15.70
16	Jeff Andretti	15.83
17	Didier Theys	16.24
18	Scott Goodyear	16.67
19	Ted Prappas	16.75
20	Willy T. Ribbs	18.22
21	John Jones	19.34
22	Hiro Matsushita	20.98
23	Buddy Lazier	21.72
24	Tony Bettenhausen	21.92
25	Randy Lewis	22.18

Combined Finishing Averages From 1979 - 1991

1	Rick Mears	7.61
2	Al Unser Jr.	8.03
3	Bobby Rahal	8.31
4	Mario Andretti	8.70
5	Michael Andretti	9.59
6	Emerson Fittipaldi	9.98
7	Danny Sullivan	10.26
8	Arie Luyendyk	11.56
9	Scott Pruett	13.07
10	John Jones	13.95
11	John Andretti	14.00
12	Mike Groff	14.96
13	Jeff Andretti	15.18
14	Eddie Cheever	15.74
15	Didier Theys	15.82
16	Scott Brayton	16.01
17	Randy Lewis	16.30
18	Scott Goodyear	16.33
19	Hiro Matsushita	16.51
20	Willy T. Ribbs	18.21
21	Ted Prappas	18.25
22	Paul Tracy	18.75
23	A.J. Foyt Jr.	18.87
24	Tony Bettenhausen	19.55
25	Buddy Lazier	19.89

Combined Starting & Finishing Averages From 1979 - 1991

1	Rick Mears	6.25
2	Mario Andretti	6.71
3	Bobby Rahal	6.86
4	Al Unser Jr.	7.93
5	Michael Andretti	8.16
6	Emerson Fittipaldi	8.62
7	Danny Sullivan	8.78
8	Scott Pruett	11.73
9	Arie Luyendyk	11.92
10	Eddie Cheever	13.35
11	John Andretti	14.08
12	Paul Tracy	15.12
13	Mike Groff	15.31
14	Jeff Andretti	15.50
15	Scott Brayton	15.86
16	Didier Theys	16.03
17	Scott Goodyear	16.50
18	John Jones	16.65
19	A.J. Foyt Jr.	17.01
20	Ted Prappas	17.50
21	Willy T. Ribbs	18.22
22	Hiro Matsushita	18.74
23	Randy Lewis	19.24
24	Tony Bettenhausen	20.73
25	Buddy Lazier	20.80

Average Championship Finish From 1979 - 1991

			Starts
1	Bobby Rahal	3.30	149
2	Rick Mears	4.15	173
3	Al Unser Jr.	5.40	140
4	Michael Andretti	6.44	129
5	Mario Andretti	6.62	163
6	Emerson Fittipaldi	7.00	119
7	Danny Sullivan	7.44	127
8	Arie Luyendyk	14.25	106
9	John Jones	15.33	35
10	Mike Groff	16.50	25
11	Eddie Cheever	18.00	34
12	Scott Pruett	18.67	35
13	Ted Prappas	19.00	12
14	John Andretti	19.80	55
15	Paul Tracy	21.00	4
16	Willy T. Ribbs	21.50	17
17	Scott Brayton	21.64	114
18	Didier Theys	21.80	44
19	Scott Goodyear	25.50	42
20	Buddy Lazier	25.50	16
21	Hiro Matsushita	26.00	27
22	Jeff Andretti	27.00	18
23	Tony Bettenhausen	28.92	91
24	A. J. Foyt	29.08	92
25	Randy Lewis	30.38	81

All Statistics Concluded After The 1991 Season Final

Driver	Age	Team For 1991	First Indy Car Start	Total Starts	Poles	First Win	Total Wins	Residence
Jeff Andretti	27	N/A	Milwaukee,1990	18	--	--	--	Nazareth, PA
John Andretti	29	Hall / VDS	Road America,1987	45	--	Australia, 1991	1	Indianapolis, IN
Mario Andretti	52	Newman / Haas	Trenton,1964	360	51	Hoosier GP,1965	51	Nazareth, PA
Michael Andretti	29	Newman / Haas	Las Vegas,1983	129	20	Long Beach,1986	24	Nazareth, PA
Eric Bachelart	31	Dale Coyne	Australia,1992	1	--	--	--	Brussels, Belgium
Fabrizio Barbazza	29	Arciero	Long Beach, 1987	15	--	--	--	Monza, Italy
Scott Brayton	33	Dick Simon	Phoenix,1981	108	--	--	--	Coldwater, MI
Gary Bettenhausen	50	Menard	Phoenix,1966	186	2	Phoenix,1968	4	Monrovia, IN
Tony Bettenhausen	40	Bettenhausen	Texas,1979	99	--	--	--	Indianapolis, IN
Eddie Cheever	34	Chip Ganassi	Miami,1986	34	--	--	--	Rome, Italy
Jim Crawford	44	Bernstein	Long Beach,1984	13	--	--	--	Tierra Verde, FL
Dominic Dobson	32	Concept	Laguna Seca,1985	37	--	--	--	Fairfax, CA
Emerson Fittipaldi	45	Penske	Long Beach,1984	119	10	Michigan,1985	13	Miami, FL
Stan Fox	39	Hemelgarn	Milwaukee,1984	9	--	--	--	Janesville, WI
A.J. Foyt, Jr.	57	Foyt	Springfield,1957	358	53	Duquoin,1960	67	Houston, TX
Scott Goodyear	32	Walker	Meadowlands,1987	40	--	--	--	Toronto, Canada
Robby Gordon	23	Chip Ganassi	--	--	--	--	--	Orange,CA
Mike Groff	30	N/A	Detroit,1990	25	--	--	--	Studio City, CA
Michael Greenfield	27	N/A	Cleveland,1990	5	--	--	--	Manhasset, NY
Roberto Guerrero	33	King Motorsports	Long Beach,1984	104	5	Phoenix,1987	2	San Juan Capistrano, CA
Dean Hall	34	N/A	Phoenix,1990	16	--	--	--	Olympic Valley, CA
John Jones	27	N/A	Phoenix,1988	38	--	--	--	Thunder Bay, Ont.,Canada
Buddy Lazier	24	N/A	Portland,1990	16	--	--	--	Vail, CO
Randy Lewis	46	N/A	Laguna Seca,1983	81	--	--	--	Hillsborough, CA
Arie Luyendyk	38	Chip Ganassi	Road America,1984	104	--	Indianapolis,1990	3	Scottsdale, AZ
Jovy Marcelo	26	Euromotorsports	Australia, 1992	1	--	--	--	Hillsborough, CA
Hiro Matsushita	28	Dick Simon	Long Beach,1990	24	--	--	--	San Clemente, CA
Rick Mears	40	Penske	Ontario,1976	180	39	Milwaukee,1978	29	Jupiter,FL
Tero Palmroth	39	N/A	Indianapolis,1988	10	--	--	--	Tampere, Finland
John Paul, Jr.	32	N/A	Elkhart Lake,1982	26	1	Michigan,1983	1	West Palm Beach, FL
Scott Pruett	31	TrueSports	Long Beach,1988	35	--	--	--	Dublin, OH
Bobby Rahal	39	Team Miller	Phoenix,1982	149	15	Cleveland,1982	20	Dublin, OH
Willy T. Ribbs	36	N/A	Long Beach,1990	17	--	--	--	San Jose, CA
Franco Scapini	28	Euromotorsports	Australia,1991	1	--	--	--	Monte Carlo, Monaco
Tom Sneva	43	N/A	Trenton,1971	205	14	Michigan,1975	13	Paradise Valley, AZ
Danny Sullivan	42	Galles/Kraco	Atlanta,1982	127	19	Cleveland,1984	15	Aspen, CO
Didier Theys	33	N/A	Long Beach,1987	44	--	--	--	Nivelles, Belgium
Brian Till	31	Robco	--	--	--	--	--	Columbus, OH
Paul Tracy	23	Penske	Long Beach, 1991	4	--	--	--	West Hill Ont., Canada
Al Unser,Jr.	29	Galles/Kraco	Riverside,1982	140	2	Portland,1984	17	Albuquerque, NM
Jeff Wood	35	N/A	Las Vegas,1983	30	--	--	--	Witchita, KS
Jim Vasser	26	Hayhoe-Cole	Australia,1992	1	--	--	--	San Francisco, CA
Dennis Vitolo	35	Nu-Tech	Miami, 1988	5	--	--	--	Golden Beach, FL

One On One With
Arie Luyendyk

Ron Weaver Photo

"The next morning when I got up I said to my wife, 'If I read the Indianapolis Star then I guess I'll know for sure that it wasn't a dream'. I was really looking forward to opening up the newspaper the next morning, not to make sure that I won it, but the first time you look at that front page... that's pretty impressive."

In his 76th Indy car race, Arie Luyendyk won the 74th Indianapolis 500. On Sunday, May 27, 1990 Luyendyk silenced any critics who were quick to point out that Arie had never won a race. When Arie won, he won big. In his sixth try Luyendyk became the 55th driver in history to have his likeness added to the Borg-Warner Trophy. At age 37, things were finally starting to take off for him. However, Indianapolis was to be the only high point of 1990 for Luyendyk and the Doug Sheirson team. At the end of the season, both Shierson and Domino's Pizza were to throw in the towl. This left the colorful Mr. Luyendyk without a ride.

Even worse, people were starting to consider his calculated Indy win, a fluke.

Driving for Vince Granatelli in 1991, Arie proved at Phoenix and Nazareth that Indy was no fluke. Despite winning two races, 1991 was viewed by Granatelli and Luyendyk as a year they just assume forget. Lack of sponsorship meant that Granatelli would be sidelined in 1992. There was no justice for this winning combination.

In a repeat of the previous year, Luyendyk found himself a free agent. But this time, there were no full time rides available. After months of negotiations (the process of sec-

uring adequate sponsorship), Arie signed a limited race contract with Chip Ganassi Racing. However disappointing this seemed to be, that's racing.

In March 1992, I get a call from Mr. Luyendyk. "Hello, this is Rick", I answer "Hello, this is Arie, Arie Luyendyk. I just called to tell you that I can do the interview". Two days later I was to give Arie a 9:00 am call for a relaxed chat. What transpired over the next 77 minutes turned out to be one of the best interviews I've ever conducted. "Okay, Arie, are you kicking back in your lazy chair?" I ask. "Yeah", the pleasant Dutch voice responds

IICR: How does it feel to be a winning driver now after so many years of coming close to victory but then having something go wrong and ruin your chances?

Arie Luyendyk: When I signed with Doug Shierson and he announced that we were going to get the Chevrolet engine, I knew right then that we were going to be really competitive at Indy. I hadn't really been running in the middle of the pack. I had been running in the first six or seven, pretty much all of the time with the Cosworth. At Indy, we had been extremely competitive in '87, '88 and '89. Of course it really wasn't possible to compete with the Chevys. When Doug Shierson announced that we got the Chevy deal I really knew that we'd be in good shape. To me it really wasn't a surprise that we were competitive. Like in '89 for example, I was running on my own with the Cosworth and I could do 219. Then I would get close to Al Unser Sr., who was running the Penske Chevy. I got in his draft and followed him for two laps and did two laps at 221. Then he'd pull into the pits and just to see the difference, I'd drive around on my own again and fall back down to 218,219. There was a big difference in the engines then in '89. I knew if I would have one I'd be right there and that's pretty much the way it turned out. It was no surprise to me. I'd always felt really comfortable at the speedway. I've always enjoyed it since I went there in '85 for the first time. I qualified easily but when you get there and you 're a rookie the place is really intimidating. You 've got to keep yourself cool otherwise you're in the wall right away. '86 we had a terrible year with the Lolas. We just never found the setup. That was the worst year I ever had there. '87 when I came back with (Ron) Hemelgarn, we ran very quick all month. During the whole month we were the quickest March / Cosworth as far as lap times. In the race, the only one who was quicker (in a March / Cosworth) was Roberto (Guerrero). I lost turbo pressure in '87 and drove

around frustrated with only 38 inches of boost. I had the speed for years but now I also have the equipment.

IICR: You said you had the speed but not the equipment, how much does the actual team come in to play? Hemelgarn was never really a Penske type organization.

Luyendyk: I' ll tell you this, when Hemelgarn went there with me in '87 and we had Larry Curry as our crew chief, I think that was the best year and crew that Hemelgarn ever had. We had a good group of guys. He blew it by not putting together a deal at the end of the year. He let Larry Curry go, he let me go because he wanted more money from the sponsorship that I had. We didn't have the quickest engines and we couldn't really get the March to work on the road courses. We were good on the ovals with Larry Curry doing the set up. All we needed for '88 was

car owner but he blew it because he's greedy. Then I put together a deal with Dick Simon at the last moment for '88. In '88 if we wouldn't have broken down in a lot of races, I would have won a few races. I was leading at Phoenix and we had a pit fire. At Indy, I was running second when (Ludwig) Heimrath decided when the light was turning green on a restart, he would get on the brakes. I'm flying through turn four and Heimrath gets totally out of the gas, gets on the brakes, he didn't think it was green yet. I ran into the back of him. I told him later, I said "Ludwig when the pace car turns its lights off, that means that we're going green, okay, that's lesson number one. Lesson number two is if you stand on the gas in turn four, don't ever get out of it if you 're not sure". He didn't have a clue. I 've had a lot of those frustrating moments. What I was

All was well in the 1987 Indy 500, until Arie bent his suspension on lap 125, finishing 18th.

Art Flores Photo

to keep going in the same direction and the team would have been really good. Hemelgarn pretty much let it all fall apart because he couldn't find the sponsorship to back up the Provimi sponsorship. After that, he just threw together deals and only showed up at Indy, just not a good deal. That was the chance that Hemelgarn had to become a good

waiting for was to get the right opportunity and team so I could put down the results. That all came together in 1990. As far as being competitive during the whole season, that really came together in 1991.

IICR: Do you feel that you still have to prove yourself on road courses?

Luyendyk: Yeah, I think you have to

prove yourself at any given race but right now I have this label that I'm really quick on ovals. It seems that people really know that when we go to a super speedway that they have to be careful and watch out for me. That's fine with me. On the street courses in 1991, we were running right up there in the first three of four. I think that I proved a point in 1991 by being competitive on pretty much all of the tracks. After Indy, I wasn't very successful in 1990 because we just didn't test. Bob Tezak took over the team and started spending money on airplanes, suites, limousines and shit like that. We didn't test and go forward as a team although the car was always reliable. The guys did a good job but the management just wasn't able to do it. We just didn't go test, we didn't develop so we just kind of got stuck. We had good races but we didn't win. It was hard for me not to back up that win at Indy. There's a lot of pressure there. To come back in 1991 and win Phoenix that really took a lot of the weight off of my shoulders. I won Phoenix, in a pretty good fashion. That particular day, to me, might have been as important as winning Indy.

IICR: Did you think that win proved that Indy was no fluke?

Luyendyk: Yeah, a lot of people say "maybe it was a fluke". Well, you saw the race, it wasn't a fluke! People still think that way if you don't back it up. The victory at Phoenix was for me in that respect as important. I ran good at Indy in 1991 but we were a lap down due to a bad spark plug but I was happy with third place. I had the fastest lap at Indy, Michigan and Nazareth too, so I must be doing something right on the ovals!

IICR: Nazareth was a strange win for you (in 1991).

Luyendyk: Oh that was a great one. Nobody knew what hit them. We knew! I think that we proved in 1991 that I could be in the hunt for the championship. In 1992 with a limited schedule, I think I'm just the odd man out.

IICR: Does that scare you to be the

odd man out?

Luyendyk: No. I really have to say...okay if I look at myself today I'm not frustrated....I'm just kind of....how should I say.... I'm kind of

This cool photo was taken in 1988, while driving for Dick Simon.

pissed off basically. With the troubles I had in 1991, we could write a whole separate story on that with Bob Tezak. I don't even want to get into that. With all of those problems going on, with the injunction on the car in Michigan, etc. etc., the lawsuits and the whole thing. To go through a year like that was hard. In 1992, I was looking at a year where I wasn't driving as much. It kind of hurt because I felt I belonged out there. I'm also realistic enough to look back and see where it went wrong. I think that it all went wrong when Doug Shierson sold the team to Bob Tezak. I don't think that I'll be the odd man out for 1993. In 1992 I'm working my ass off for 1993. You have to be positive about it because there's no point in sitting back and feeling sorry for yourself.

IICR: After you won Indy, what kind of doors did that open for you as far as endorsements? Did that get the ball rolling for you?

Luyendyk: Well no, it didn't really do that. What I noticed, and of course it wasn't hard to notice, was that after winning Indy I had an incredible amount of recognition. Just stepping into planes and restaurants, all of these people just recognize you. I guess that might be because of the way I look. I look a little different than the average race car driver. I got real busy with the media and doing interviews, going on TV shows and doing all those kinds of appearances. I also got busy doing appearances for the sponsors that we had at the time; Dominos Pizza, Total Petroleum, Provimi, Dutch Boy and Marlboro. I did a lot of appearances and made some extra money with that but it certainly wasn't what people say. People say that everyone's going to stand in line to give you money and endorsements. It wasn't like that, it really didn't happen. If I look back at the other winners, I don't think it happened to many guys. I saw some commer-

After a haircut, Arie tests for a new team, at Laguna Seca in March, 1990.

cials with Bobby Rahal and Rick Mears but those were all commercials with companies who were involved with the teams that they drove for. I didn't see that happen to other drivers and it definitely didn't happen to me. As far as winning the race and giving me the recognition, that was incredible. Especially for me, since I hadn't won any races. To the public I was like this surpise. But people who knew the racing business knew that one of these days he's going to win a race. For me that was the best thing that could ever happen to me.

IICR: It's like when "Big Al" won his fourth Indy, he won and then went home to Albuquerque and that was it.

Luyendyk: I think that you really have to have a guy, a hustler to go after that for you. Not after you win it, before you win it. I was somewhat prepared in 1990. I had worked with a guy named Randy Shwar. I met him Phoenix and kept in touch with him by phone. I called him a week before Indy in 1990. I said "I need your help. If I win Indy here next

At Milwaukee in 1988.

standing there waiting for you to come back to the Goodyear garage to watch you do the post race interviews. So here comes Arie Luyendyk

Luyendyk came close to his first victory at Portland in 1988, but went home empty handed.

week, which is possible,I'm going to be busy". So I told him " watch the race, be prepared to get your ass out here when I win the race"! He watched the race and he was in Indy the next day. It was kind of a premonition I guess.

IICR: After you won Indy, I was

on a golf car and you 're kicking back like it was just another day of practice. I thought to myself, "Man, this guy should be doing circles after winning the big one". You didn't really seem that excited.

Luyendyk: Yeah, well I guess that's just me. My character is that of, you

know, I'm not an extrovert, I'm kind of an introvert in a sense. I get along really well with people, I talk to everybody. It was also a little bit overwhelming. All of the suden, you know, you say to yourself "f*ck, I finally won this thing !" It's not that I didn't realize what was going on but still it's very overwhelming. You remind yourself that this race is not that easy to win. I've done it and it's incredible. If I win a race, I don't jump up and down and go nuts. That's me anyway and I was just sort of overwhelmed.

IICR: How many days does that take to sink in ?

Luyendyk: I guess the next morning when I got up I said to my wife " If I read the Indianapolis Star then I guess I'll know for sure that it wasn't a dream. I was really looking forward to opening up the newspaper the next morning, not to make sure that I won it but the first time you look at that front page... that's pretty impressive. During the race, the last couple of laps when I was touring the track, I wasn't nervous. I wasn't worried that maybe something would go wrong with the car. I was really confident after passing Rahal for the lead. I don't know, I get this thing into me where I just say to myself, "nobody's going to take this away from me now". I get very aggresive and very mean. I would have done anything to block a guy coming up to pass me for the lead. I wasn't over-whelmed when I was in the car and I was actually leading the race. I was quite confident and comfortable. But then when you get out and you have thousands of people cheering you on, that's overwhelming. That's just something that you dream about. You know, when you're on the plane and you close your eyes when you're flying somewhere you just kind of think to yourself "that would be cool". Late in the race, I was starting to pull away (from Rahal) a lot. I just kept going hard because I never wanted him to get the impression that he was coming back at me. When you 're in the car and you gain some on the guy in front of you, you seem to get more out of yourself. Then you're into the fight. If you're leading and can pull out a second a lap, the guy behind you gets that message too. It could work to demoralize the guy. That's what I wanted to keep doing, keep putting distance between him and myself. To him, to say to himself "it's over". Everybody had troubles that day with blistered tires. We had two sets of blistered tires. My last set was blistered and I didn't even realize it. The car was pushing like hell and it was vibrating. It started to vibrate immediately so I thought it was the balance. As it turned out, it was the blisters. I was worried about it be-cause the car was vibrating and I thought "Shit, I hope this isn't some-thing major". The last ten laps were pretty long.

IICR: You won in a very calculated fashion. Is that just something you learn from experience?

Luyendyk: At the speedway, yeah. You figure to yourself that it's a long race so what you 've got to do is stay on the lead lap. The radio communi-cation between Doug (Shierson) and I was so good. I knew exactly the whole race how far Emerson (Fittipaldi) was ahead of me and everybody else in between, how far they were ahead of me. In my mind, I could picture where they were on

Arie posing with the Dick Simon crew before the start of the 1989 Indy 500. Engine failure would end his race.

the track. Like when I crossed the start / finish line, Doug would say "You 're minus 20 (seconds) behind Emerson". So I knew that he's on the middle of the back straight now, and everybody else is in between. I was always there in the hunt. Then with the car, the way it was working we had made some wing adjustments and changed the stagger, we got the car to work really well because it was pushing for the longest time in the beginning of the race. After we got it right, then I just started flying. Then, it's like you get wings. Now, I was catching the guy in front of me by a second a lap. You can see him come closer. You drive like you 're driving in quali-fying, flat out all of the time. Even though we were like 25 seconds back in sixth place, I knew that during the next pit stop I needed to make a change to make the car handle better. If that would happen, then

I knew that I would make up the time. We didn't fall into it, it hap-pened for a reason. When the time was there to go for it the car was at its best. That's what every driver really dreams about, is to have a car that good at the time when you need it. Rahal was doing high 219s

Always one to appreciate the limelight, Arie gives his signature to yet another fan.

and I was doing high 221s and 22s.

IICR: You were running less wing angle than Rahal.

Luyendyk: We ran less downforce then most of the guys during the race. The less you drag on the straightaways, it's really going to help you.

IICR: Growing up in Holland, I assume that you had dreams of a Formula 1 career? Is this correct?

Luyendyk: Yes that's true. If you know Holland, it's a small country but we've got a lot of big companies, major companies that could sponsor and support drivers to go to Formula 1, except the unfortunate thing is they don't do it. The racing in Holland is just not a sport that is supported. To get to Formula 1 you need bags of money. You need talent but you need bags of money too. I just never got into that situation. Formula 3 is the stepping stone to Formula 1 and I never really got the right program because of budget problems. I was competitive in Formula 3 but I never was a dominant race winner. To get to Formula 2, which was at that time the step before Formula 1, I was never able

to get the budget to do that at all. So my dream of getting to Formula 1 just could have never have materialized. When I came to the States at the end of 1980, I was invited to do a super vee race at Phoenix. That was my first oval experience. I drove Peter Kuhn's back up car. He had an old Ralt RT-1 as a back up which was a flat bottomed car. I drove that car and finished sixth. I was happy with my performance and so were other people so I got a ride for 1981. To make a long story short, when I came to Phoenix and I saw the Indy cars, something just kind of clicked in my mind. All of the sudden, I just turned all of my attention to the American racing scene. I said to myself "if I can't get into Formula 2 or even Formula 1, then this is what I want to get into, the Indy cars".

IICR: Was that a scary decision to pack up everything and move to America?

Luyendyk: No. As a kid when I was three years old my dad moved to South Africa. When I was ten, we packed up and went back to Holland. I was pretty much used to traveling around. Racing in Europe,

we just traveled all over the place. We slept in the back of a van and worked on the cars together, so I was pretty much used to the rough life. In 1981, I did the super vee series which was the year that Al Unser Jr. won the championship. I flew back and forth to Europe. When I got in touch with the Provimi people and they started to sponsor me at the end of 1983, I decided, to be successful, I had to be here all of the time. I moved over here at the beginning of '84. I did a full year of super vee and won the championship. That same year I was given my first race in an Indy car at Elkhart Lake through the Provimi team and Aat Groenevelt. I had no problem moving over. Especially not the way that the Provimi people set things up for us. They were fantastic. We moved into a nice apartment and they gave us a car to use. They used to have a private company plane then and we flew in the company plane to almost all of the races. We were winning races and leading the championship, it was like a dream. That was a dream year. Then getting into an Indy car before the

Arie poses with crew and family the morning after winning the big one.

Steve Weaver Photo

season was over, to think that the year before I had nothing, I had no ride, I had nothing. Things can change around quickly if you get the support. That's the kind of support I never really got in Holland. That's why I was never able to make it to Formula 1.

IICR: How frustrating is it to go to all of the major corporations in Holland and have them turn you down? Do you still try ?

Luyendyk: I feel sorry for the guys that want to make a career right now in Holland. Believe it or not, it's myself and Jan Lammers. He and I, for the last 15 years are the drivers representing Holland. There are no new faces coming along except Cor Euser who drove at Laguna for Bettenhausen in '91. He's another guy. He's really quick, he's really good but he just doesn't get the support. One of these days it might happen for him but he's way into his thirties. For all of us, we've all had to struggle like hell. We all have to struggle in America too ,whereas ten years ago the struggle wasn't that hard to get a ride.

IICR: I once read where Geoff Brabham said that driving Indy is 90 percent boredom and 10 percent terror. Is that pretty close to the truth?

Luyendyk: Well....I never get bored at Indy, believe me. It could be the other way around, it could be 90 percent terror if the car is a piece of shit then that's what it's like. If the car is good during the race and you can race hard, but you always have to keep in the back of your mind that you cannot overdrive the car. If you do, the track will beat you and it will eat you. You have to have respect for the track and you have to know your limits. If you don't know your limits and that of the car, you 're going to go into the wall. If you look back on the last few years, it's usually the same guys that end up in the wall.

IICR: Why do you think that is? Do some drivers just not get a feel for the car?

Luyendyk: I don't know. You have

Thanking Chevrolet, the new Indy winner poses with car owner Doug Shierson.

Luyendyk comes in for his final pit stop of the 1990 season at Laguna Seca.

Steve Weaver Photo

Art Flores Photo

to have a good feel. If the car doesn't want to accept full throttle then it's not going to. It doesn't even matter what type of line you use. You have to keep working with the car to make it work. The driver cannot overcome deficiencies of the car at Indy. The driver can't really make up for the deficiencies of the car anywhere, road courses or ovals, because the other guys have their shit together so they 're going to beat you.

IICR: What's your favorite race track?

Luyendyk: It's kind of hard to say. I really enjoy Elkhart Lake. That's way up there on my list. I 've come to enjoy racing at Michigan. As far as

pure racing fun, I think that Michigan is up there with Indy as far as fighting it out with a bunch of cars and driving wheel to wheel. That's pretty much what I enjoy about racing, the competition. Actually getting out there on Sunday and racing against the others. That is what I get the most enjoyment out of.

IICR: What's the most difficult track in your mind?I've heard that Phoenix is pretty tricky.

Luyendyk: No, I don't think it's Phoenix, but that's easy for me to say because I 've won there. That's another place, when the car is not right, you can scare the hell out of yourself all day long. If the car's right then it's great. Again you 've got to

67

know your limit. When I won there in 1991, the wind was blowing like hell and it shifted the limit. You 've got to be able to adjust on all tracks. I think that the street courses are the hardest courses. It's so easy to be a second slower on the street courses because if you let off a little bit on any turn or not get on the power all you can, you come in the pits and say "Why the hell am I a second off". Then you go out and try just a little bit harder and you 've got it. You have to be really agressive on the street courses. You have to be really precise because you have such little room to work with.

IICR: Do you like the street courses?

Luyendyk: Yeah, I like them. I like them because they 're so challenging. You 've got to sit down and go for it. What I even like more about the street courses is when it rains. I've always done a lot of racing in Europe in the rain. I really enjoy driving in the wet. Then you can really show some skill. The set-up is important but you can make up a lot of time by driving well.

IICR: In your mind who are the best drivers in the rain?

Luyendyk: Emerson is quick in the rain. Michael, Little Al. There are more than just those three guys but they come to mind right now.

IICR: When you strap yourself into the car is it about the same level of excitement or nervousness at each track?

Luyendyk: I guess it's more a matter of the adrenaline flowing in your body. You're getting ready for a challenge. I think the most nervous I get, if you want to use the word nervous, I don't really get nervous

You get little butterflies and you get a little tense. That's usually for qualifying more so than the race. I always look forward to the race. Then you can get all of the testing, practicing and qualifying out of the way and go and have some fun in the race. That's the fun part, going out and trying to beat the other guys. For me, that's the biggest part of racing. Maybe that's why I usually end up better on race day rather than qualifying.

IICR: Is the adrenaline flowing faster

Luyendyk and the rest of the drivers will surely not miss the old Detroit circuit.

like on a super speedway where you're really going quick?

Luyendyk: No, it's pretty much the same everywhere.

IICR: Is it an awkward feeling for you after you started winning races and the photographers and reporters were all over you ?

Luyendyk: To me, I kind of like that. Not that I like to have my picture taken but to me that's like you 've accomplished something and now it's being recognized by the outside world. It's kind of a good feeling. Going back to Indy in 1991, I was really looking forward to it. It was a lot of fun to go back. Now people expect you to do well again. That really wasn't a problem at all. I had no nerves or any tension within me that I wouldn't have been able to

live up to the expectations of 1990. It doesn't get in the way of doing my job. Up until I walk up to that fence where all the fans are I'll sign a few autographs and then I can get on with the job with the car. I can easily shut off all of the other stuff when I get into the car. Except when it's like two minutes before the race I get pissed off when somebody comes up to me and wants an autograph! I can't understand that this person doesn't understand that I would like to have a minute to myself. It's like anything. When you write your book and I read it and say "Rick, I think that you did a good job". I'm sure you feel better about that then if I say "Rick, I think that you did a lousy job". I think we all need a little patting on the back. The fan and press recognition is a little bit of a patting on the back for us.

IICR: At Indianapolis, do you look forward to "happy hour" (the last hour of practice) and going out there and cranking off some 225 MPH laps?

Luyendyk: (Laughing) Yeah I do I think it's great. A lot of team owners don't think so. I love to do that but on the other hand I say to myself, "Don't get carried away". It's not important but I just like to do that for one or two laps and then park it. It doesn't make you any money but it just feels good. That's what you 're there for. You want to go as quick as you can without putting the thing into the wall and hurting yourself. It's a competition. At the end of the day you 're actually competing for the honors. That's what makes "happy hour"

68

That's what makes "happy hour" fun.

IICR: Do you get a little more intense when you know it's five o'clock?

Luyendyk: No, not at all. It's happening in a very relaxed way. You say to yourself, "I can do it now, relax". I keep saying to myself, "Why should I get nervous before qualifying. I can do it at any given time, so why shouldn't I be able to do it on qualifying day". I kind of psych myself that way to make it a lot easier on myself. It usually works out well that way to not be nervous.

IICR: When you're running that fast at the speedway, what's the main thing that you notice as far as changing track conditions? A driver once told me that the turns get so fast that it's like one long turn instead of two different turns.

Luyendyk: Really, right now, there's no such thing as the 'short chute'. It's like one big corner, that's true. You're in the short chute for so little time that it's hardly going straight. The car is going straight but not for long. The track gets narrower and narrower. That's why you see everybody running that low. We have to run low to go that quick.

IICR: When you do go low do you figure that the shortest way around a circle is by taking the line through the inner circumference?

Luyendyk: I've tried it both ways, it doesn't work. The speeds were identical. When you go through the corner and you're down that low, when you come off the corner and you still have the car low, in other words you don't come close to the wall. What you're doing is you're enforcing the car to scrub off speed because you're turning the wheel. You have to free the car up to make it maintain its revs coming off the corner. I just use the whole track. I go down low and then I let the car go all the way up to the wall as close as I can get. I've experimented with all kinds of lines and to me the old fashioned 'use the whole track' line still works the best.

IICR: Do you ever notice the crowd when you're driving at Indy?

Luyendyk: No, it's amazing. You drive on that track and you don't notice the crowd. What you see is the concrete wall and the track. You don't really look over to the crowd. It's like a wall of people. I'm not trying to pick out who's sitting where! Sometimes you smell the barbecues in the infield that's kind of interesting. The thing that bothers me is the shit laying on the race track. The paper and the cups, that stuff can

Same helmet, different car and team, Detroit 1991.

ruin your race if it gets into your radiators. I guess there's no way to control that.

IICR: Okay, it's the end of the day and you hop into your rent-a-car, is that an awkward feeling having to go from 225 MPH to maybe 40 or 50 MPH on the drive back to the hotel?

Luyendyk: No, it's not. No matter how you look at it, after running around Indy for a number of laps during the day, it's like you let everything go. You let your whole body relax. You say "Okay, the day's over so now I can relax". It's not like you have to keep going fast in your road car. I have to admit that 55 (MPH) is really bad! It's so slow! (laughing) 70 would be better. But I guess with the way some people drive I guess maybe 55 is best.

IICR: Have you ever been cruising down the road and have somebody look over and recognize you and

they kind of freak out?

Luyendyk: Yeah, that happens. At Indy it happens a lot. I've had people jump out of their cars at a stop light to get an autograph. I have to laugh about it. Then they have to get back in their car and the light's green so everybody behind them is pissed off!

IICR: I've heard a lot of drivers say that they don't like driving on a full stomach. Is that true with you?

Luyendyk: For me it's true. I eat very lightly before a race. But you have to eat something because you have to give your body fuel so to speak. When I work out, it's like driving in the car. I eat something in the morning before I work out and I always eat something before a race. Like at Indy, when I wake up I have a pretty good breakfast. I might just eat a sandwich before the race, nothing heavy. Usually I eat bananas because they're easy to eat and I like them. I'm usually standing there by the car before the start with a banana in my hand.

IICR: How much of your private life gets lost after you win Indy? Are there times when you're asked to do something and think to yourself, "I'd really rather be spending time with my wife and family"?

Luyendyk: That definitely happens. A lot of times, when I'm on the road and I'm doing an appearance I say " I could be doing a lot more fun things with my family than signing autographs". But that's part of the job and just the responsibility that's there with the job. Indy, for me, is three weeks of work, but I enjoy it. After driving, my routine is that I usually go to the health club and work out till about eight then have dinner. After that I just go back to my room and relax. I usually stay at the Lees Inn on Lafayette Road. I work out at the Scandanavian Health Club. After driving during the day it's kind of good to go to the health club.

IICR: If you don't work out frequently and let yourself go, then get back in the car, do you really notice it?

Luyendyk: No, because during the season I don't really work out that much. You do enough driving. Your body needs enough time to recover from a race. Like when you race at Detroit, you're f*cked for three days. You've got to let your body recover. I take fluids and do some stretching. I don't work out for three days after Detroit because my back ,neck, legs, feet, arms hurt. Also your hands have blisters. You lose all this weight and your body needs to recover. The winter is when I really work out every day. I try to work out five of six times per week.

IICR: Do you have an office somewhere or do you have an office at home?

Luyendyk: I had an office built on to my house. It's about 400 square feet. I can close the door and it's like I'm in my own office. I always try to be organized so I'm always busy in my office every morning I'm home. I've got a bunch of files, I keep pretty organized. Pretty much, I get up at about eight o'clock, I get a cup of coffee then i'm on the phone till about twelve or one o'clock. After that, I go work out. During that time in the morning, I do paper work. Funny enough, I have a lot of paper work. I just got a computer so that I can document all of my expenses so that I don't have all that work at the end of the year.

IICR: You really like living in Arizona.

Luyendyk: Oh yeah, I think it's the best. The weather is so nice. What my wife and I like to do is work on our home. All of the time that we're at home we're in the house. We built on my office and we do a lot of work in the yard. We keep pretty busy. They've got great schools here. My son (Arie Jr.), he's ten, he goes to public school.

IICR: Tell me a little bit about your art gallery.

Luyendyk: In '88, I bought an art piece by this Dutch artist Frank Gude. I got to meet Frank and I really liked his work. I came to Arizona in 1990 and we were talking. He had done quite a few oil pieces on Indy car racing. So he says, "Maybe we should open a gallery. I'll make the art". So I said " Yeah, that sounds really neat". So I just did it pretty impulsively. It cost me quite a bit in the beginning. Right now it's going quite well. I just thought that it was a fun thing to do. I collect art. I'm not a high end collector of art, I just collect a little art. I like things that people make. I'm kind of in to that. That's why I enjoy having the gallery. If I didn't have that then maybe I would be bored.

IICR: Do you look at art, as an investment?

Luyendyk: Well, the art I have, some of it is mine and some is on consignment. When I started I never looked at it and said "This is what I want to do for a business". It's heading into that direction. I don't know if I'll keep the gallery forever. I did it impulsively and I still kind of work at it that way.

IICR: Do you still own that old Provimi Indy car?

Luyendyk: Yeah, I have the 1985 car that I drove at Indy. I might be doing some more collecting of cars that I drove. It's something that I'm pursuing. I don't know what I'm going to do in the future but whatever type of business that I have, whether it's retail of it's a dealership or something, then I could have a section where I could pull of this

racing memorabilia. It would just be a nice thing to have in any kind of business just to make it attractive.

IICR: Okay, here's a fun one. You're obviously into music. Who are some of your favorite groups?

Luyendyk: If I had to give you a list of the kinds of CDs I have, it goes from Anita Baker to Whitney Houston to Guns & Roses. So you can see that I'm pretty flexible in my taste. I like the new Guns & Roses album. The Cure and Depeche Mode, I kind of like that English type of stuff.

IICR: Are you into heavy metal at all?

Luyendyk: No, not really. Guns & Roses, I thought that they did a few good songs but I'm not really into heavy metal. I'm not a headbanger. Michael Bolton and Mariah Carey I like their stuff.

IICR: No Metallica, huh?

Luyendyk: No.

IICR: Have you ever met any of these musicians?

Luyendyk: I just met Vince Neil (ex lead singer of Motley Crue) last week. He's going to run the ARS (Indy Lights) cars. He's a great guy. There's another guy I know who plays with Melidian, Dave Clark Howe. He's a big fan of mine and he's really a nice guy. They're trying to get a record contract. Their music is great but they need support. It's just like in racing.

IICR: If you could play an instrument, what do you see yourself playing?

Luyendyk: I always had an ambition to be a drummer but I didn't have any talent. I tried it once and I didn't have a clue. I don't have musical talent. It's too bad.

IICR: You mentioned earlier that you know that you don't look like the traditional race driver. What's it like to go to those former winners parties at the speedway or the Leaders Club(a club open exclusively to drivers who have led a lap during the Indy 500) and you find yourself standing there next to Rodger Ward or Parnelli Jones or Foyt or whoever and here you are, this long haired foreign guy. Does that make you feel really different?

Luyendyk: (laughing) No not really. I don't really see it that way because when I'm in a group of people like that I'm just one of them. I'm a race car driver and I can relate to them and they can relate to me. In that respect we're all the same. I always chuckle because here are guys that are retired that I used to read about. I'm thinking that one of these days this kid is going to show up and he'll say to me, I always used to read about you and he's going to beat my ass! I have to chuckle when I go to those occasions.

IICR: Do you ever think to yourself after all the good things that have happened to you in America, like that Russian comedian used to joke "what a country". Do you ever think about that?

Luyendyk: (laughing) I do, yeah. I came over here when I got the sponsorship from Provimi and I got a good super vee deal. I won the championship and got an Indy car ride that year and the next year I'm running at Indy. This all happened pretty quickly after I'd been strug

gling for eleven or twelve years in Europe. So to me, if anybody in Holland ever dares to say anything bad about America, I get pissed. I take it personally because this is the place where it happened for me. That's something that is a part of me now. I don't even feel like I'm not from America. To me, I'm just one of the cast. You know like Mario is an American now, I'm getting closer to feeling that way. I'm still Dutch and I don't know if I'll become a citizen. I might do that. I really don't have to because I 've got a green card. I'm legal! This country still has a lot more opportunity then a lot of other places in the world. For instance, when I opened my art gallery, all I had to do was lease the place, hire somebody to run it and hang some art. In Holland, you have to go through so much shit before you can do that it's ridiculous. I think it's a great country and my wife thinks so too. We don't have any intentions of going back to Holland. My daughter, I talk to her in English. I don't even bother with talking Dutch because that's what they learn in school. My son understands Dutch a little be

cause when we came over he was two years old and we had been talking to him in Dutch all of the time. He can understand most of what I say. My daughter, she's an American -- she was born in Milwaukee!

IICR: At 38, how many more years do you see yourself driving?

Luyendyk: Well I know one thing, I'm not going to keep on going as long as A. J. has. I think if you have the desire age isn't as important. You have to have the desire but you also have to have the physical strength to do it. I think that Mario has that still. I think he's the only driver who's older who has that, in my opinion. To go around Indy for 500 miles and be quick, you don't need as much physical strength or stamina as you need to drive at Detroit for two hours. There's no comparision in the physical aspect of the two. I think that Mario is the only one who can still do both. If I can do that, I'll be racing for a long time. If I had to guess, I don't know, four or five more years. I think 45 is a nice age. But then again I 've been saying that for a long time!

□

Wearing USAC number 1, Arie went on to take third place at Indy in 1991.

Doug Wendt Photo

One On One With
Bobby Rahal

"Money had nothing to do with it. Some people attribute it to that. Any driver worth his salt, I mean you want to make as much money as you can but there's not enough money in the world to get you into turn one at Indy when you're flat out at 235 MPH. You've got to want to do it and you have to be with a team and a car that you think can do it".

The Indy Car Racing media guide perhaps says it best when describing Bobby Rahal, "always a threat to win". During his 10 years Indy car career, Rahal has won 20 races. Bobby Rahal is a driver's driver, taking a very methodical road to the big time.

It all started back in 1973 when 20 year old Robert Woodward Rahal started in his first SCCA amateur race. The best move at the time was to the Formula Atlantic series, where he won the championship. In the later part of the '70s, Rahal proceeded to compete with the late, great Gilles Villeneuve in the Formula Atlantic series. The next move was to the now defunct Can-Am series.

In 1981, Rahal moved to IMSA, with a win at the 24 hours of Daytona. During his climb to the top, Rahal hooked up with an astute businessman named Jim Trueman. Trueman was the owner of Red Roof Inns, which is the largest privately owned hotel chain in America. Teaming up with Trueman would eventually see the talented Rahal enjoying Indy car success, the kind of success that leads to financial security.

In the later years, Rahal began investing his money in car dealerships, planting the seeds of early retirement. Then there were dreams of owning his own Indy car team. That dream became reality in December, 1991. Political events of the sport caught up with Pat Patrick, owner of Patrick Racing for over 23 years. Rahal was given the opportunity to buy the Patrick team. But Rahal needed financial help to put the deal together. That help came in the form of longtime friend, Carl Hogan. Hogan, a Chicago businessman, had built a trucking empire and was looking for new areas to conquer. In teaming with Hogan, Rahal now has the kind of stability that eliminates the many surprises a driver can stumble upon, especially late in his career.

Before the Australian race in 1992, I talked with Rahal about the current state of Indy Car Racing, his past and present.

IICR: So tell me how much responsibility is it to be a part owner of a team? Is it easier or harder than you expected?

Bobby Rahal: Well, I never expected it to be any trouble at all. Frankly, I'm probably doing as much work as always, slightly more. I guess why it doesn't seem to be any more trouble is the fact that because I have a direct voice in the direction of the team and a direct role. Before, things could be frustrating because I was asked to do so much and then in the end had no control or direction, at least certainly nothing when it really came down to a major decision. Now I do, so consequently I think what in reality is more work seems to be less. I don't know if that makes sense to other people. Having the vested interest with Carl, having the direction and control over the destiny of myself and the team, in the end it feels much less demanding than maybe before.

Can - Am was one of Bobby's steps up the ladder. Here he is at Laguna Seca in 1981.

During his rookie season, Rahal won twice, a rare accomplishment in Indy car racing.

IICR: What were some of the first things that you learned if any?

Rahal: I don't think that I've really learned anything more. Looking back to when I first started at TrueSports with Jim Trueman, my responsibilities were a lot more than just driving the car. I think that any driver since the late 1970's, unless you've got a famous name, you had to really go out and hustle the business side. There's been very few that I think have had a lot of doors just opened to them. A lot of drivers have had to go out and really work the corporate side. As a result, I would say that most of the later day drivers that have made it have had to be involved in the business side of it all along. I don't know if I've learned anything more other than now, I have the opportunity to apply what I have learned over the years.

IICR: How far back did you start thinking about owning your own team?

Rahal: I'd say probably about two years ago. Two to three years ago. To be honest, I certainly never intended to do this, this quickly. I thought that there was just no way, because of my position in the automotive world. In terms of having a number of (automotive) dealerships and obviously one day wanting to have more, to be more involved with the corporate world, having a team started to make more and more sense. Certainly as a driver, having direct control over what I drove as I got older seemed to appeal to me more. I'm not reliant on a team per se. How many good drivers have we seen either not be in the right equipment or be "retired early' because they didn't have any control over their future? As I got older I did not want to leave my career to the whim of fashion! It just seemed to make more and more sense as time when along.

IICR: So tell me what those CART INDY CAR RACING meetings are like?

Rahal: Well, they're different! It's nice to be on the inside looking out, I can tell you that. I think that CART INDY CARS have taken a lot of criticism that is undue. Obviously there are problems. There are things to be solved, there are directions that have to be taken. I think that it's performed very well. The traditionalists may not like it because it's not all on ovals. But the last time they raced on that type of schedule, Indy car racing was about dead, back in the late 1970's. There are certain people in the press and what have you that may not be happy about it

74

but I think the reality is that CART's done a helluva job, particularly in a bad economic climate. I think that it's been less effected than many of the other series. Formula 1 is in far worse shape than CART is, in terms of its financial strength. NASCAR, there a lot of deals there that I understand aren't what they seem to be. In the CART meetings there's a lot of comment, a lot of dissertation, there's a lot of argument. But I think that there is a general understanding of what everybody wants CART to be: the premier racing organization in the world. People have different ideas on how to get there, but at least they have ideas. At least I have a voice and a vote in that. It can be looked at as being very frustrating but it can also be looked at as being very positive.

IICR: Do you think that the situation really isn't as bad as it seems in the press?

Rahal: Well, I think it depends on which press you talk to. There are some people in the press that seem, to me to have it out for CART. Then there are others that are very supportive of it.

IICR: Why do you think it's like that?

Rahal: Well, It seems that some people in the press have just as big of an ego as race car drivers or promoters or what have you! If their feathers get ruffled they're going to fight back. Don't get me wrong, it's not that there aren't issues that need to be taken care of. No matter what 's going on, or however frustrating it may be to have 24 voices, I think that in the end that it's the way to go.

IICR: What do you think of all of the tension between CART and the (Indianapolis Motor) Speedway?

Rahal: I think that if nothing else, if we don't all sit down and realize that we need each other, I think we're all a bunch of fools and we'll all lose in the end. We need Indianapolis and Indianapolis needs us. We just have to put away the egos and it has to be give and take. I think that (Speedway President)

Tony (George) has valid points and I think that CART has valid points. If it wasn't worth anything then there wouldn't be all of this argument would there? I guess if nothing else it's a reflection of the value of what INDY

At Laguna Seca, 1983.

CAR RACING is all about. If it was nowhere, if it wasn't successful, if there wasn't a lot of money in it, nobody would care one way or the

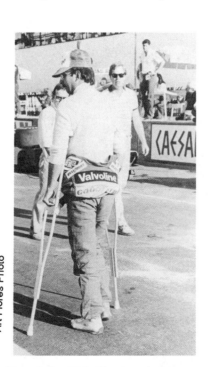

The only time Rahal has been hurt in an Indy car came at Caesar's Palace in 1983.

other.

IICR: You've said in the past that sometimes your business enterprises were starting to take a toll on

your driving career. How do you balance both, being a business man and a full time race driver?

Rahal: Number one is that I'm very fortunate that I have very good people around me. That really gives me the ability to do all of these things. If I did not have the kind of people that I have as my partners there would be no way. It was some of the other things, things that were really taking a lot of time that really weren't of value. I sort of have to remember what got me to where I am. Not that I'd forgotten that but racing is what got me here. Racing begot the dealerships the new team, you name it. It's just a matter of reducing some of the "noise" as I call it. Concentrating on the things that are most meaningful. That means not doing IMSA races and things like that. As much as I like IMSA, it's time consuming and in the end at this stage... I don't mean to belittle IMSA racing but it doesn't really do anything for us at this stage. It's much more important for me to test, for example, to spend two days testing our Indy car than it would be to go run an IMSA race. The impact if we go out and win an Indy car race because of that, then that's our main area of discipline. We have to really concentrate on that. It was never really that bad, I just sort of had to reduce a lot of the "noise" and concentrate on what got me here.

IICR: When you left TrueSports at

the end of 1988, it didn't seem to be a very friendly departing. What were some of the reasons you left? Was it because you were stuck with the Judd engine?

Rahal: I left because when Jim Trueman died (June 1986) I think my... I won't say there's a power play but I think that I just didn't fit within that organization anymore. Mrs. (Barbara) Trueman and Steve Horne had ideas as to how the team should be run and I guess that I had ideas. As a result, I just didn't feel as though I had a home there anymore. It was difficult because Jim and I had basically started it, I had to go out and do a lot of things to make it happen. It never could have been done without Jim anyway, but I had to find people to buy the cars and engines. I just felt that I really didn't belong there anymore, my role had changed. As a result, as difficult as it was to even think about leaving, I felt that I really didn't have much of a choice.

IICR: There were also rumors that you left to pursue more money at Galles / Kraco. Was that a consideration?

Rahal: Not at all. I mean, I made a lot of money at TrueSports because we won a lot of races. In fact I'd almost say that I won more, I made more money at TrueSports than I

did at Kraco that first year, because we won a lot of races. Money had nothing to do with it. Some people attribute it to that. Any driver worth his salt, I mean you want to make as much money as you can but there's not enough money in the world to get you into turn one at Indy flat out at 235 MPH. You've got to want to do it and you have to be with a team and a car that you think can do it. Some people attributed the move to that. Those who did A): didn't know me and B): didn't know the situation anyway. It's always easy to point at money as being the rude cause of everything, but in reality it's usually one of the last causes.

IICR: You mentioned that you realize that you have to have all of the right equipment to make things work, but how do you approach that now that you're signing your own pay

Rahal with Steve Horne at a Laguna Seca test in 1987. Bobby quit smoking in early 1988.

check?

Rahal: Well, you just know what it takes over the years. You know that we have to have an adequate budget, you know that we have to do all of these things to attract the right

Dueling with Al Unser, Sr at Michigan in 1986.

kind of sponsors. I think that you have to have a vision of where you want the team to be not just today but tomorrow and beyond tomorrow. You have to have the right kind of people within the team. If you're the right kind of leader you can attract the right kind of people. That's based not just neccessarily on being able to pay the most money. One thing, TrueSports was never one of the biggest payers for crews. Especially when Jim was there, there was an atmosphere that just attracted the best people because they knew that there was a seriousness about winning. Jim was alway a great believer that you can not buy loyalty. Loyalty comes from action. There were always people bouncing around from team to team making the most money. But the team never really benefited from it and neither did they. The way I've approached this is to recapture, in many respects, a lot of the lessons I learned from Jim in how to motivate people. That's by giving them a direction, a leadership, giving them theopportunity to go beyond the very narrow definitions of their job. I think that we're building that right now. Whether it's the right cars or the right engines or computers. We signed a deal with Digital Equipment that from a technical side is a tremendous help to us. It's not just money, it's products and services and advice and what have you. To me, the key to the future in Indy car racing for our team is to have access to technology. That should put us ahead of the ball game.

IICR: Looking back at your college education, you have a degree in history from Denison University. How did you

Steve Weaver Photo

In 1986, Bobby wins Indy on his fifth try.

go from being interested in history to being a race car driver?

Rahal: Well, when you're in a liberal arts college it almost doesn't matter what you major in. I did not go to college thinking that I was going to become a professional race car driver. In fact, when I went to college I doubted that I would drive a race car anyway because even though

my father had raced, it was not... you know if you did it, you did it for fun. You had to go out and get a job first. My plan was to go to law school or do something, I wasn't really quite sure what I wanted to do. History was as good as anything and it's something that I enjoyed. I might just as well have majored in home economics because there's obviously no connection to the racing world. More than anything, I would tell any young fellow or woman who wants to go into racing, as a driver or what have you, to get your education. Believe me, if you cannot carry yourself, if you cannot converse, if you don't have an interest in the business world, if you're starting from dead center

Art Flores Photo

Leading at his favorite race track, Road America, in 1987.

where you don't have a name to help you go over the early hurdles, you've got to go out and sell yourself. I think that an education does a lot in helping you do that.

IICR: Looking back, do you regret not majoring in business?

Rahal: I took economics, you have to. I could've majored in Econ II but I just had to pick one or the other I guess.

Rahal joined Kraco Racing in 1989, with limited success. This is a pit stop at Cleveland.

IICR: Back when you started driving Indy cars in 1982, especially after you won your first race at Cleveland, here was Bobby Rahal being exposed to America, and a lot of people said "This guy sure doesn't look like a race car driver". Was there any effort to change your image at any time over the 1980's?

Rahal: Well, I guess that I never really knew what it was. Certainly I 've shown that I can go as fast as anyone. I think that the press are the ones who keep talking about me being balding and bespectacled. They 've always got to come up with some kind of a label for you. If I don't fit the mold as some people perceive it, that's fine with me. Somebody will say " You 're losing your hair". Well, Sterling Moss didn't have a lot of hair

nor did Fangio nor a lot of other drivers. If we're so vain that everybodies got to fit an image then I don't want to be part of that image anyway. I frankly think that my image as being different works in my favor. The old adage " You can't judge a book by it's cover" I think that's perfect for me. Corporate America responds to that. I may not have girls hangin' around, but that's fine with me. I'm a married man. I'm

Bobby is united with new teammate, Al Unser, Jr. in his first test with Galles / Kraco at Laguna Seca in late 1989. The two still remain good friends.

happily married with a family, I don't need any of that...stuff. I'd much rather be respected by the chairman of the board of some company than having girls knocking on the door of

my hotel room at all hours or whatever.

IICR: After you won Indy in '86 did you see the demand for your time really start to escalate?

Rahal: I think so, sure. Winning Indianapolis, like I 've said to people, no matter how little people know about racing they know Indy. It just opens things up for you that you would normally not have available.

IICR: Okay, lets go back to when you had won Indy and then the next year you go back and all of the sudden, unlike previous years, there's all kinds of photographers and reporters around you. What was that like?

Rahal: Hey, I can remember when they weren't there. I 'd much rather have them around. It's a reflection of the job you 're doing. I've spent enough time in racing to know the down times to know good times when I see them. Like when people ask for my autograph, it wasn't that long ago when people didn't even want it. I don't understand the sort of conceitedness that some people carry

because they 've achieved something that means they're better than everybody else. I don't think I'm that kind of person.

IICR: Is there that same sort of magic

after you win the championship?
Rahal: Not from an outside standpoint. From an internal point, from inside me, I think that winning the championship is more meaningful because you just know how much effor, on a day to day basis. has gone into acheiving it.

IICR: Does it upset you that people always remember who won the Indy 500 but a lot of them forget who won the championship that year?

Rahal: I think that's beginning to change a little bit. Remember, how long has Indianapolis been around? It's just like Le Mans in France or the Masters in golf or the U.S. Open in tennis. There's too much history and tradition and Americana wrapped up in it to expect a series of other races to equal it. If Indy had only been around for five or ten years then it would be a different story.

IICR: When did you open your own private office; Bobby Rahal Inc.? Did you do that because things were really starting to happen financially?

Rahal: I opened it in 1987. I did it mainly from not only a financial standpoint but also I felt that when I was going to be leaving TrueSports, I had always had an office in the corporate offices of Red Roof Inns. Jim always wanted me there. When Jim died, there was just sort of a sense that they needed that space. I started to distance myself a little bit. One way that I did that was to have my own office somewhere else. It was a good move for me.

IICR: It must be indespensible for you to have a full time secretary who keeps track of everything for you ?

Rahal: I couldn't do it without her

(Linda Lett). Just from a scheduling standpoint because I'm traveling around so much, I need to have someone that everyone can call at just about any time. People call to see where I'm at and what I need, or can I be here, can I be there. I've got to do it. It's very hard to find a secretary who can do it. Linda used to be

At Long Beach, 1991.

one of the secretarys for one of the principal officers of Red Roof. She's great, and she's tough !

IICR: Do people ever just walk in to your office and say " Can I have an autographed picture"?

Rahal: No, because we don't advertise where we are.

IICR: Do you have your own airplane?

Rahal: Yeah, it's a Beach Baron. I got it in 1990. I take it to all of the close races or business trips. Taking it to California really doesn't make much sense. It's great because I'm home in a couple of hours. With my schedule being as full as it is I don't have the time anymore to sit around on Monday or Tuesday and wait for a commercial flight. It's a great time saver. It allows me to visit my dealerships on a regular basis. I couldn't do as many things if I didn't

have the plane.

IICR: When you started the dealerships was there the idea that not only would racing make a good sales tool but also an entertainment tool for some of your clients?

Rahal: Oh sure, absolutely. At the races we've had the major executives of Honda, Toyota, Oldsmobile some of the companies that we represent. At Nazareth we entertain the people that work for us, the salesman and mechanics and their families. We invite around 120 people to Nazareth. It's a way to say thanks to them for doing such a great job. I'm not inventing any of this, I just look at how Roger Penske has done it and just sort of follow the dotted lines.

IICR: Do you have a Suite at the (Indianapolis Motor) Speedway?(These cost about $60,000 per year to rent)

Rahal: Yeah, we have one of the new ones on the inside front straightaway. Again, I've done some things in the past with a view towards the future. The suite was one of them. I asked PlastiKote to help me with it. I felt that this was a good thing in the future to entertain our clients, to sort of take care of the corporate side. It's been a great thing for me and I think that PlastiKote has enjoyed it. In fact, we're looking for another one.

IICR: Does it ever get to be inconvenient at times when people notice you in public?

Rahal: Not really, most people are pretty good. Most people are respectful, it's kind of fun talking to them a little bit. Most people are really supporters of mine. I've never had a bad instance where somebody's come up to me and said "I think you're a piece of junk" or" I hate you". It's nice that people take the time to say "hi" to me.

IICR: Is it kind of refreshing to maybe meet someone who has no clue who you are?

Rahal: Oh, sure. My ego doesn't need that. I don't need to have people recognize me. In (Dublin, OH) people recognize me all the time. If I'm on the road and somebody doesn't recognize me, I don't care. I remember a couple of years ago, I was at the Columbus airport and this guy comes up and I was busy and sort of thinking elsewhere. This guy comes up and says " Hi my name's Jay Leno and I just wanted to say I'm a fan and I'm in town" and blah blah blah. So I say, "Nice to meet you" and blah blah blah and it didn't even click in my head. So I get on the plane and I'm looking through a *Time* magazine and there's an article on Jay Leno in it ! I said to myself " Holy smoke" I felt like a real jerk! (laughing) There are all kinds of people that I don't recognize so I wouldn't expect people to recognize me all of the time. I don't want then to anyway

IICR: What's it like appearing on *The David Letterman Show* ?

Rahal: It was great. I still talk to David. In fact, I think he might become a part of our race team. He's always expressed a desire. He's become a good friend. He's been to a number a races with us over the last few years.

IICR: What's your favorite race track on the circuit?

Rahal: It's really hard to say. I guess the one that I've always loved, I never could get tired of driving, is Elkhart Lake.

IICR: What about the (Indianapolis Motor) Speedway?

Rahal: I mean, I like the speedway but I'm a road racer. The speedway can be a lot of fun. You're there so long that it becomes work after awhile. Day in day out, I think that Elkhart Lake is someplace that

I could never get tired of racing at.

IICR: What's your least favorite?

Rahal: Probably, it's gone now, was the last version of the Meadowlands. I won twice there so I guess I should have loved it, but I thought that it was pretty unimaginative.

IICR: What about the street courses in general?

Rahal: I like the street courses in general. I think they put a real demand on a driver's abilities.

IICR: What do you think is the hardest race track to drive as far as being hard to figure out? I've been told by other drivers that Phoenix is real hard.

Rahal: Phoenix is the most frustrating place in the world. It's sort of screwy. There's been races that I've gone in thinking the car felt real good and we've had miserable days, and then I've gone in there thinking

feel for the car or the track in general? What do you think?

Rahal: I don't know. I think especially with the ovals the worst thing you can do is let your ego rule you. You're going too fast for that. If the car isn't capable of doing it then you work with it until it does. It takes a pretty strong driver to say "Hey, I'm just not going to run it any harder". Especially when other people are going fast. You want to prove to everybody that you can do it. I think that you make mistakes, mental mistakes. You overrule your judgements.

IICR: Have there ever been times when you were practicing at the speedway and had the mechanics make a change, then go out and come back in and say "We better go back to the way it was before because I almost fenced it"?

Rahal and Carl Hogan take time for a photo shoot during Rahal-Hogan's first test at Phoenix in 1992.

that this is going to be a long day and I won one race once and finished second in the other. I love it, it's as challenging as you can get but I don't know if you can ever feel confident that you've got it all set up.

IICR: Like at the speedway, it seems like certain drivers always crash a lot over the years. Do you think that the driver just doesn't have the right

Rahal: I don't know if I've done it from an ego standpoint, but you've got to be willing to try different things too. You've got to do it progressively. You just don't go out and make a huge change without not knowing what the hell's going to happen. At Indianapolis discretion definitely is the better part of velor.

IICR: When you do make a change at Indy how fast do you have to get up to before you can feel it?

Rahal: Well, I think that you 've got to get up to where you were before to know if it's going to be any better or any worse.

IICR: How fast before you can start feeling the ground effects start to work?

Rahal: Oh I don't know, it's hard to say. Probably as soon as you 're going about 50 MPH you should start to feel it, but you don't feel the car suck down to the ground or anything, at least I never have. You 're so low anyway. We are talking about such small measurements....you just know when it's right and when it isn't.

IICR: A few years ago when there was the white line controversy, (at Indianapolis concerning drivers running below the white line on the bottom of the track) did you guys just fugure out that the shortest way around a circle is by taking the inner circumference line?

Rahal: Oh sure, absolutely. Not only that, you don't have to turn the wheel as much. The difference between your average speed at Indy is the difference between your top speed on the straightaways and your slowest speed i n the corners.The more you turn the steering wheel the more speed that you scrub off. So if the corner's wider, if effect less radius, then you don't have to turn in so much so you're not scrubbing as much speed. It's simple why everyone was running down there.

IICR: What have been some of the best Indy cars that you 've driven over the years as far as models?

Rahal: The '86 March was a good car, the '85 March was a very good car. Adrian Newey did both those cars. The '90 Lola was very good. The '89 Lola was pretty good. A lot of it had to do with the tires. The tires in '87 were awful so the '87 Lola felt horrible at Indianapolis but it felt a lot better than most of the Marchs did. The '86 March was very predictable, at least ours was. You knew exactly what it wanted between qualifying and race forms. The '85 March was the same, very consistant. The '90 Lola was extemely good, the '91 was not that much better. I think that the '92 was a big change and much better than the '90 or '91 Lolas.

IICR: How many years did it take you to really understand how to set up an Indy car and how everything reacted?

Bobby Rahal the businessman.

Rahal: I don't know, I'm still finding that out. I don't think that you ever really know.

IICR: In your opinion as far as support series, what's the best route to take to make it to the big time?

Rahal: It's hard to say. Unlike many sports there's so many ways of getting to the top. Mears came from off road racing I came from road racing. Some guys come from sprint car racing although very few nowadays. Some guys came from IMSA or you name it. There's any number of ways to skin the cat. I definitely think that the (formula) Atlantic is a very good series to make it to the Indy cars. The best advice to give would be to run a series that you can afford. If you can't afford to run the entire series, then you can compete for the points championship. That's not going to do you any good to just run a few races here and there. The (Indy Lights)..... I'm not sure if that's the best way. Alot of drivers run a few (Indy Lights) races and that's it.

I think that you need to go out and compete in the whole series to get any kind of name recognition.

IICR: How's your golf game been?

Rahal: Not that good. All of my business commitments keep me from playing a lot of golf. I live on a golf course but I very rarely play at home, I'm never there, I usually play on the road.

IICR: Overall what's the best part of your job?

Rahal: I think the variation. The different people, it's never the same day, the same thing. It's a very demanding lifestyle but on the same token I wouldn't trade it for anything. My life is never boring. I doubt there are many people who can say that about their job. The biggest down side is being away from home.

IICR: When you retire, do you see yourself running a few races after that like running just at Indy every year?

Rahal: No when I retire I will not drive another race car. I will take over the day to day control of the team.

IICR: Looking back on your past, who are the most important people that got you to where you are?

Rahal: My father (Michael)and Jim Trueman. Without my father having been a racer, even though an amateur one, I would have never been interested. He gave me the opportunity and supported me early on. Of course, Jim Trueman...without Jim, God knows where I'd be. ❑

The Secret To Success

The technology battle in Indy car racing has led to new angles of attack. In Rahal - Hogan's case, these are mostly front and rear wing angles. As part of the buyout of Patrick Racing, Rahal - Hogan took over the team's research and development facility near Poole, England. Just a few miles down the road from the Penske factory, the crew at Rahal - Hogan are forever tinkering with their 1/3 scale wind tunnel model. Aerodynamic testing is the sole purpose of the shop's existence

" I think that it's an ego thing to say that you have a shop in England, but we don't treat it that way", comments part owner Bobby Rahal. "Our facility in England is not there to produce parts, we can do that in Indianapolis. We are trying to take advantage of the expertise that is over there".

The U.K. shop is managed by Mike Clark. Mike was once a Penske engineer who left to start his own aerodynamic consultation business. One day in September, 1990, the phone rang and Clark was told that Patrick Racing was in search of someone to head their research and development program.

Could such a shop be located in the United States? The answer is yes, but there are certain things to consider as Clark points out. "There are a couple of things that we have to look at:A) there's a difference in the technology availability in the U.K. B) with the contract that we have with Lola, we have to use the same wind tunnel. This assures accurate results. To be able to have access to this valuable information, Lola wishes to have control over their models. They've been here, they've walked around the place, they know where we are. If they allow people to rent their models, then if the models are being shipped around the World, they've got no idea that confidentiality is being retained ".

Clark explains how the team arrived at having the extra advantage of conducting private wind tunnel testing. " Basically, Rahal-Hogan has a contract with Lola Cars to purchase two chassis, with an option on a third, which is usually taken. Part of the contract is that the team has a supplemental agreement that provides for a wind tunnel program. The team pays a deposit for the hire of wind tunnel models and the receiving of certain drawings and information. As part of the agreement, we use the same wind tunnel (Cranfield) and equipment as Lola".

Most manufacturers use a 1/3 scale model to develop a new car. The same size model is used to further fine tune aerodynamics by Rahal-Hogan.

" Essentially, we have two 1/3 scale models that were made in 1991. Under the contract, we were given a set of drawings to change the '91 models to '92 specifications. The reason why we have two models is that one is in road course trim and the other is in super speedway configuration. This saves time and money by not having to change everything around during the actual test ".

All of the wind tunnel testing in the World doesn't matter if a team can't relate the results to the race track. Clark explains how all of the testing back in England benefits the race team. " To try and improve the car's performance on the track, you have to understand how the car is performing aerodynamically in all sorts of attitudes and different speeds. If you have a back up of information that tells you what you can expect to happen, then the race engineer has roughly 1/3 of his job done. The engineer is in the situation where he can relate to the driver and the wind tunnel information. He can then relate to problems and use the wind tunnel information to overcome them. Essentially, after a test, I'll get the raw data. I then speak to Steve Newey, who is the team's race

engineer. We then verbally discuss any significant gains ".

Testing various wing angles and ride heights in the wind tunnel, translates into less work for the team back in the States. Rahal explains, "It's a lot better to test in the wind tunnel because we don't have to conduct the same tests all day long in practice. We go to the race track knowing that if we run a certain rear wing, we know what we have to do with the front wings and etc. That means that we can do other things with the limited time that we have in practice. It allows us to have background or a foundation of knowledge that should allow us to do a better job at any race. We'll spend about 7 or 8 days in the wind tunnel devoted to Indianapolis settings alone".

How does all of this information reach the actual race team?, Clark explains. " We send the small drawings by fax. The large drawings go by Federal Express".

Of course, this jump on the competition does have a large price tag. Rahal gives a hint of the annual price of this investment. " It's well into six figures, it's over $500,000.

Unit J-22 is home to Rahal - Hogan's England shop. At first glance, the shop resembles a fire station !

Acknowledgments

Bill Allee
Ian Bisco
Andrew Broadley
Mike Blanchet
Steve Bunkhall
Mike Clark
Linda Cummings
Bill Donaldson
Nick Goozee

Paul Harcus
Robin Hostetler
Mario Illian
Linda Lett
Arie Luyendyk
Steve Miller
Alan Mertens
Paul Morgan
Line Page

John Potter
Denise Proctor
Bobby Rahal
Wally Reese
Gere Schneider
Dan Taylor
Malcolm Tyrrell
Martin Webster
Colin Whittamore

Edited By Jill Taylor

Photographers

Rick Amabile
Dan R. Boyd
Bob Ellis
Art Flores
Brian Spurlock
Ron Weaver
Steve Weaver
Doug Wendt

Design & Arrangement
By
Rick Amabile

Additional Information

C.A.R.T. Media Guide
Cosworth Creative Power,
By Ken Wells
Indianapolis News
Record Book
Indianapolis 500 Year-book, 1975,1980-1991,
Hungness Publishing

Written Jan -- Mar, 1992
Clovis, CA

About The Author

Rick Amabile is the grandson of the legendary two-time Indianapolis 500 winner, Bill Vukovich. Born in Fresno, California, Rick has been addicted to Indy car racing since the age of 13. He began working in Indy car racing part-time for team VDS, while still a junior in high school.

Amabile went on to work with various teams including the winning Kraco team, before going on to pursue other interests. Rick stays close to racing by working for Premier Industrial Corp. in its Gasoline Alley service room each year during the month of May.

Rick is also the author of *The Insiders Guide To Indy Car Racing* and *Inside Indy Car Racing, Volumes 1 and 2*.

Inside Indy Car Racing is an annual publication with different features each year.

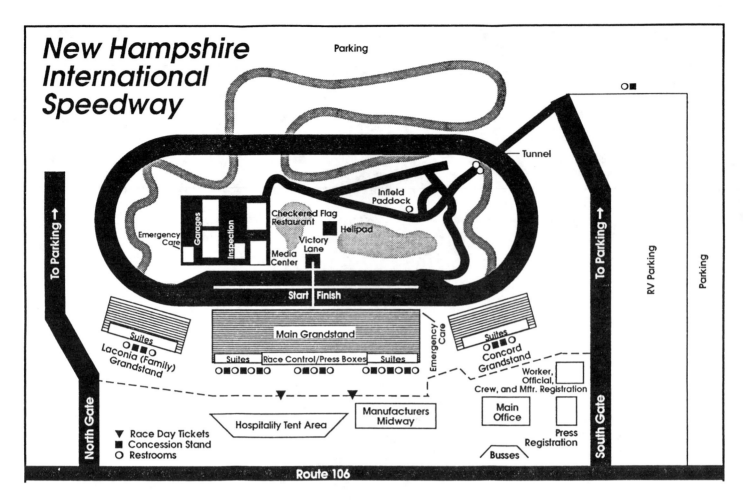

New Hampshire International Speedway

Parking

Tunnel

Infield Paddock

Checkered Flag Restaurant

Helipad

Emergency Care

Garages

Inspection

Victory Lane

Media Center

To Parking →

To Parking →

RV Parking

Parking

Start Finish

Main Grandstand

Emergency Care

Suites

Suites

Suites

Race Control/Press Boxes

Suites

Laconia (Family) Grandstand

Concord Grandstand

Worker, Official, Crew, and Mftr. Registration

North Gate

▼ Race Day Tickets
■ Concession Stand
○ Restrooms

Hospitality Tent Area

Manufacturers Midway

Main Office

Press Registration

Busses

South Gate

Route 106

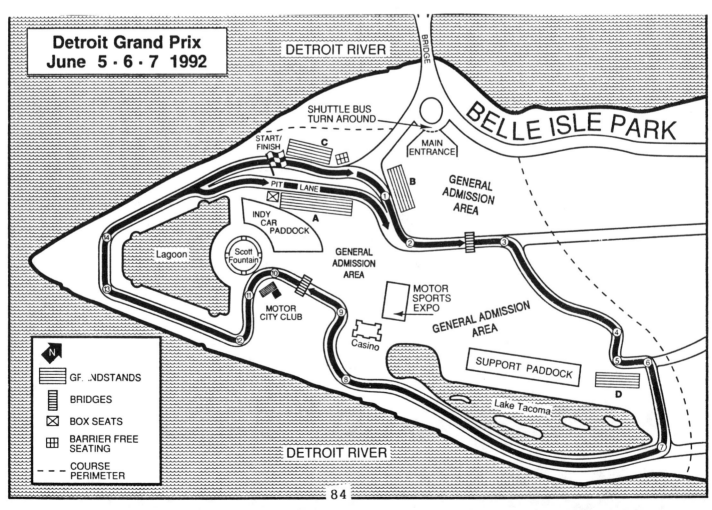

Detroit Grand Prix
June 5 · 6 · 7 1992

DETROIT RIVER

BRIDGE

BELLE ISLE PARK

SHUTTLE BUS TURN AROUND

START/FINISH

C

MAIN ENTRANCE

PIT LANE

A

B

1

GENERAL ADMISSION AREA

14

INDY CAR PADDOCK

Lagoon

Scott Fountain

GENERAL ADMISSION AREA

2

3

13

10

MOTOR SPORTS EXPO

11

MOTOR CITY CLUB

9

Casino

GENERAL ADMISSION AREA

4

12

SUPPORT PADDOCK

5

6

8

D

N

GRANDSTANDS

BRIDGES

BOX SEATS

BARRIER FREE SEATING

COURSE PERIMETER

Lake Tacoma

7

DETROIT RIVER

Four Fingers

The only four-time Indy winners

A.J. Foyt, Jr. 1961, 64, 67, 77

Rookie age:
23

Age at first victory:
26

Age at last win:
42

Time span of victories:
16 years

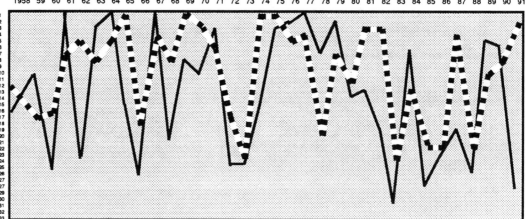

Al Unser, Sr. 1970, 71, 78, 87

Rookie age:
26

Age at first victory:
31

Age at last win:
48

Time span of victories:
17 years

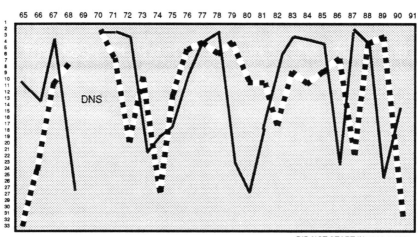

DNS

DID NOT START IN 1969 & 1991

Rick Mears 1979, 84, 88, 91

Rookie age:
26

Age at first victory:
27

Age at last win:
39

Time span of victories:
12 years

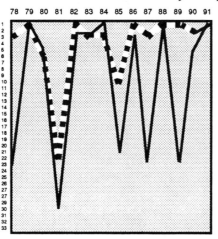

Indicates Starting
Position

Indicates Finishing
Position

	Average Career Start	Average Career Finish
A.J. Foyt, Jr.	9.71	13.56
Al Unser, Sr.	10.92	10.44
Rick Mears	4.14	10.14

1984 PPG INDY CAR WORLD SERIES
DRIVER PERFORMANCE CHART

	DRIVER	STARTS	RUN AT FIN	TIMES LED	LAPS LED	LAPS COMP (2286)	MILES COMP (3945.44)	POINTS	PURSE
1.	Mario Andretti	16	11	23	572	2000	3389.977	176	$931,929
2.	Tom Sneva	16	12	25	480	2074	3610.732	163	632,331
3.	Bobby Rahal	16	12	20	485	2156	3706.067	137	559,900
4.	Danny Sullivan	16	10	7	158	1782	3028.535	110	552,426
5.	Rick Mears	11	9	13	273	1403	2815.127	110	730,329
6.	Al Unser, Jr.	16	9	7	79	1764	2945.867	103	435,715
7.	Michael Andretti	16	11	6	48	1958	3362.928	102	433,852
8.	Geoff Brabham	16	12	0	0	1859	3122.607	87	416,356
9.	Al Unser	16	9	7	20	1734	3048.278	76	386,181
10.	Danny Ongais	13	6	2	6	1458	2497.711	53	211,829
11.	Roberto Guerrero	16	6	1	2	1176	2279.473	52	405,536
12.	Howdy Holmes	16	9	1	8	1866	3267.801	44	235,393
13.	Josele Garza	14	8	1	14	1612	2938.874	42	291,992
14.	Gordon Johncock	13	9	1	1	1677	2930.685	39	249,137
15.	Emerson Fittipaldi	9	5	0	0	935	1415.041	30	175,582
16.	Jacques Villeneuve	9	7	3	50	1045	1391.542	30	105,737
17.	John Paul, Jr.	7	5	1	10	645	1334.500	28	118,547
18.	Al Holbert	14	4	0	0	1138	2206.751	28	287,693
19.	Derek Daly	11	5	0	0	966	1811.967	26	194,542
20.	Chip Ganassi	8	4	0	0	799	1290.289	24	164,185
21.	Pancho Carter	5	2	0	0	900	1679.250	22	94,558
22.	Johnny Rutherford	6	3	1	46	906	1498.524	20	115,758
23.	Scott Brayton	13	9	0	0	1528	2800.282	19	170,209
24.	Kevin Cogan	9	4	1	6	889	1603.744	17	144,464
25.	Teo Fabi	7	3	3	15	637	1048.580	15	165,199
26.	Dick Simon	14	8	0	0	1523	2610.799	15	237,998
27.	Jim Crawford	3	1	0	0	162	275.730	12	42,240
28.	Corrado Fabi	4	2	0	0	409	406.038	11	58,059
29.	Pete Halsmer	12	6	0	0	1122	1940.687	9	157,333
30.	Chris Kneifel	6	3	0	0	553	1028.965	9	140,277
31.	A.J. Foyt	5	1	1	15	656	1283.000	8	89,712
32.	Herm Johnson	3	1	0	0	405	735.500	5	81,373
33.	Bruno Giacomelli	2	1	0	0	102	192.420	5	24,013
34.	Arie Luyendyk	1	1	0	0	48	192.000	5	14,380
35.	John Morton	5	2	0	0	513	927.770	5	70,128
36.	Ed Pimm	13	3	0	0	1011	1630.696	5	114,091
37.	Gary Bettenhausen	4	3	0	0	674	1244.435	3	35,771
38.	George Snider	1	1	0	0	193	482.500	2	69,357
39.	Dennis Firestone	5	2	0	0	528	987.910	1	79,779
40.	Michael Chandler	1	0	0	0	58	96.860	-	9,800
	Roger Mears	1	0	0	0	10	10.000	-	6,080
	Johnny Parsons, Jr.	1	1	0	0	129	129.000	-	1,080
	Tony Bettenhausen	4	2	0	0	579	1223.500	-	91,507
	Tom Gloy	3	0	0	0	289	656.460	-	68,667
	Patrick Bedard	1	0	0	0	55	137.500	-	56,793
	Spike Gehlhausen	2	0	0	0	204	430.500	-	56,291
	Stan Fox	5	0	0	0	339	468.100	-	76,885
	Jose Romero	1	0	0	0	0	0.000	-	2,000
	Ken Acheson	1	0	0	0	4	6.728	-	8,417
	Graham Hill	1	0	0	0	23	57.040	-	1,400
	Randy Lewis	3	0	0	0	117	204.060	-	22,243
	Dick Ferguson	5	0	0	0	75	227.920	-	18,101
	Steve Chassey	7	1	0	0	389	886.300	-	103,229
	Chet Fillip	3	2	0	0	329	751.500	-	6,051
	Phil Krueger	1	0	0	0	88	176.000	-	1,805
	Bill Alsup	3	1	0	0	530	885.548	-	33,869
	Ludwig Heimrath, Jr.	1	0	0	0	8	32.000	-	6,737
	Jerry Karl	2	0	0	0	51	121.000	-	8,952
	Dale Coyne	1	1	0	0	67	159.700	-	2,880
	Peter Kuhn	3	1	0	0	140	264.100	-	9,680
	Mike Nish	1	0	0	0	102	102.000	-	6,333
	Michael Thackwell	2	0	0	0	146	209.975	-	26,126
	Desire Wilson	-	-	-	-	-	-	-	4,174
	Bill Tempero	-	-	-	-	-	-	-	4,800

1985 PPG INDY CAR WORLD SERIES
DRIVER PERFORMANCE CHART

	DRIVER	STARTS	RUN AT FIN	TIMES LED	LAPS LED	LAPS COMP (2051)	MILES COMP (3758.258)	POINTS	PURSE
1.	Al Unser	14	12	14	322	1747	3353.071	151	$843,885
2.	Al Unser, Jr.	15	9	16	210	1620	3008.678	150	730,242
3.	Bobby Rahal	15	9	22	467	1621	2877.388	134	595,811
4.	Danny Sullivan	15	10	14	209	1787	3199.071	126	958,063
5.	Mario Andretti	14	6	19	514	1701	3084.472	114	714,246
6.	Emerson Fittipaldi	15	11	7	55	1629	3208.120	104	587,895
7.	Tom Sneva	15	8	6	23	1619	2879.298	66	321,053
8.	Jacques Villeneuve	11	5	1	14	948	1497.499	54	215,854
9.	Michael Andretti	15	6	2	29	1221	2349.408	53	363,454
10.	Rick Mears	5	3	3	36	629	1219.000	51	245,177
11.	Johnny Rutherford	14	8	6	36	1441	2698.744	51	378,519
12.	Josele Garza	15	8	2	31	1345	2202.584	46	289,963
13.	Ed Pimm	13	10	1	1	1587	2841.853	45	285,297
14.	Kevin Cogan	15	8	1	15	1534	2729.218	44	297,856
15.	Geoff Brabham	15	8	0	0	1430	2470.472	41	326,556
16.	Pancho Carter	10	7	2	18	1258	1994.000	37	256,454
17.	Roberto Guerrero	14	3	6	49	1155	2259.998	34	360,850
18.	Arie Luyendyk	12	7	0	0	1064	2007.682	33	298,248
19.	Bruno Giacomelli	9	3	1	3	739	1339.153	32	168,233
20.	Jim Crawford	7	4	0	0	622	1119.506	16	169,865
21.	Bill Whittington	9	4	0	0	687	1448.396	15	198,794
22.	Scott Brayton	10	3	1	1	845	1623.140	15	228,112
23.	Alan Jones	1	1	0	0	50	200.000	14	31,864
24.	Danny Ongais	6	3	0	0	637	1212.240	14	120,062
25.	Howdy Holmes	12	7	0	0	1255	2499.273	12	256,756
26.	Jan Lammers	5	2	1	5	401	671.261	11	54,965
27.	Michael Roe	4	2	0	0	264	484.866	11	56,067
28.	Roberto Moreno	5	2	2	13	251	550.874	10	55,972
29.	Johnny Parsons, Jr.	1	1	0	0	198	495.000	10	98,862
30.	Raul Boesel	10	4	0	0	597	1347.923	10	207,149
31.	Enrique Mansilla	3	1	0	0	329	548.926	8	36,997
32.	Pete Halsmer	4	3	0	0	445	675.886	7	37,965
33.	Steve Chassey	8	4	0	0	856	1666.328	6	113,910
34.	Dennis Firestone	10	2	0	0	872	1565.262	5	124,995
35.	Rupert Keegan	3	1	0	0	218	418.000	4	13,116
36.	Dick Simon	7	3	0	0	770	1361.552	3	146,148
37.	Chet Fillip	3	2	0	0	415	675.440	3	11,237
38.	Dominic Dobson	2	0	0	0	163	798.680	2	26,223
39.	Herm Johnson	2	1	0	0	65	226.900	1	15,768
40.	Derek Daly	1	1	0	0	189	472.500	1	77,962
41.	Randy Lanier	9	2	0	0	484	964.168	–	51,334
	Spike Gehlhausen	2	1	0	0	315	442.000	–	17,612
	John Paul, Jr.	2	1	0	0	246	613.360	–	71,112
	Phil Krueger	2	0	0	0	203	468.500	–	12,453
	Rocky Moran	1	1	0	0	80	133.600	–	17,988
	Tom Bigelow	3	0	0	0	408	670.000	–	35,190
	Ian Ashley	1	0	0	0	49	87.416	–	3,330
	A.J. Foyt	6	0	0	0	252	465.912	–	70,135
	Don Whittington	3	0	0	0	216	447.500	–	87,979
	Gary Bettenhausen	2	0	0	0	127	121.432	–	24,727
	Chip Ganassi	2	0	0	0	190	440.500	–	62,060
	Dale Coyne	5	0	0	0	60	144.000	–	85,036
	Sammy Swindell	2	0	0	0	97	213.500	–	29,289
	Rich Vogler	1	0	0	0	119	297.500	–	71,182
	Jeff Wood	1	0	0	0	36	89.280	–	2,040
	Dick Ferguson	1	0	0	0	4	6.680	–	4,320
	Chico Serra	1	0	0	0	29	55.535	–	2,640
	Ludwig Heimrath, Jr.	1	0	0	0	12	27.700	–	1,840
	Tony Bettenhausen	1	0	0	0	31	77.500	–	63,612
	George Snider	1	0	0	0	13	32.500	–	53,262

1986 PPG INDY CAR WORLD SERIES
DRIVER PERFORMANCE CHART

	DRIVER	STARTS	RUN AT FIN	TIMES LED	LAPS LED	LAPS COMP (2434)	MILES COMP (4250.948)	POINTS	PURSE
1.	Bobby Rahal	17	11	25	436	2116	3669.076	179	$1,488,049
2.	Michael Andretti	17	11	29	699	2150	3758.940	171	953,597
3.	Danny Sullivan	17	12	11	211	1959	3285.960	147	815,653
4.	Al Unser, Jr.	17	14	8	75	2188	3782.358	137	764,646
5.	Mario Andretti	17	11	13	204	1886	3078.762	136	700,636
6.	Kevin Cogan	17	9	8	81	1900	3196.998	115	739,719
7.	Emerson Fittipaldi	17	8	6	72	1634	2775.708	103	587,888
8.	Rick Mears	17	8	15	229	1594	3095.060	89	725,991
9.	Roberto Guerrero	17	7	8	200	1557	2602.088	87	560,502
10.	Tom Sneva	17	3	7	111	1588	2640.622	82	423,431
11.	Johnny Rutherford	17	13	5	105	2049	3540.530	78	549,868
12.	Geoff Brabham	17	9	2	3	2020	3473.706	64	464,693
13.	Raul Boesel	17	11	0	0	2098	3700.478	54	430,023
14.	Josele Garza	12	7	0	0	1244	2440.778	45	374,184
15.	Jacques Villeneuve	13	6	0	0	1047	1905.800	38	308,161
16.	Roberto Moreno	16	5	1	7	1554	2888.708	30	313,062
17.	Arie Luyendyk	15	6	0	0	1381	2424.688	29	352,719
18.	Ed Pimm	12	6	0	0	1284	2167.593	29	296,701
19.	Pancho Carter	4	2	0	0	773	1560.748	28	174,948
20.	Randy Lanier	9	6	1	1	1009	1759.860	21	268,331
21.	A.J. Foyt, Jr.	8	2	0	0	996	1863.816	16	166,354
22.	Jan Lammers	5	3	0	0	471	690.426	13	80,842
23.	Derek Daly	3	2	0	0	345	562.116	11	64,436
24.	Randy Lewis	8	4	0	0	512	965.622	8	140,336
25.	Johnny Parsons	8	2	0	0	722	1007.974	8	186,814
26.	Spike Gehlhausen	3	2	0	0	376	763.000	6	29,036
27.	Chip Robinson	2	1	0	0	180	313.878	6	32,340
28.	Ian Ashley	3	1	0	0	167	359.080	4	30,720
29.	Sammy Swindell	1	1	0	0	187	467.500	4	15,051
30.	Dominic Dobson	9	1	0	0	482	962.912	3	173,564
31.	Mike Nish	3	1	0	0	124	232.221	3	38,128
32.	Dale Coyne	8	2	0	0	343	577.329	2	168,540
33.	Gary Bettenhausen	8	2	0	0	709	1288.028	2	220,992
34.	Rick Miaskiewicz	6	3	0	0	411	641.390	2	54,964
35.	John Morton	1	1	0	0	97	172.660	1	20,104
36.	Rocky Moran	8	1	0	0	324	649.842	0	126,057
	Al Unser	5	1	0	0	532	1029.980	0	121,775
	Dennis Firestone	5	1	0	0	323	568.000	0	83,515
	Scott Brayton	5	0	0	0	361	737.500	0	129,247
	Dick Simon	4	1	0	0	233	560.438	0	119,376
	Jeff MacPherson	4	1	0	0	154	394.400	0	56,660
	Steve Chassey	3	2	0	0	294	414.000	0	41,636
	Desire Wilson	3	1	0	0	178	447.500	0	43,630
	Chip Ganassi	2	1	0	0	329	555.500	0	92,421
	George Snider	2	0	0	0	119	293.000	0	89,856
	Danny Ongais	1	0	0	0	136	340.000	0	79,713
	Rich Vogler	1	0	0	0	132	330.000	0	90,563
	Tony Bettenhausen	1	0	0	0	77	192.500	0	77,713
	Jim Crawford	1	0	0	0	70	175.000	0	95,263
	Phil Krueger	1	0	0	0	67	167.500	0	82,413
	Tom Phillips	1	0	0	0	8	15.200	0	7,120
	Eddie Cheever	1	0	0	0	2	3.568	0	14,620

1987 PPG INDY CAR WORLD SERIES
DRIVER PERFORMANCE CHART

DRIVER	POINTS	STARTS	RUN AT FIN	TIMES LED	LAPS LED	LAPS COMP (2067)	MILES COMP (3778.202)	PURSE
1. Bobby Rahal	188	15	12	13	315	1794	3123.050	$1,261,098
2. Michael Andretti	158	15	10	16	459	1792	3119.140	937,074
3. Al Unser, Jr.	107	15	8	1	12	1512	2610.411	732,000
4. Roberto Guerrero	106	12	7	17	273	1470	2857.166	762,361
5. Rick Mears	102	15	9	3	80	1496	2828.980	661,152
6. Mario Andretti	100	15	5	18	610	1542	2817.873	922,162
7. Arie Luyendyk	98	15	11	1	3	1815	3226.940	514,615
8. Geoff Brabham	90	15	9	5	14	1686	2980.882	501,934
9. Danny Sullivan	87	15	9	2	5	1605	3018.823	645,615
10. Emerson Fittipaldi	78	15	7	7	209	1545	2837.116	565,637
11. Josele Garza	46	15	10	0	0	1664	3087.944	407,565
12. Fabrizio Barbazza	42	14	7	0	0	1580	2825.558	465,733
13. Al Unser	39	5	2	1	18	808	1601.300	655,559
14. Tom Sneva	38	10	5	0	0	964	1589.301	355,379
15. Derek Daly	27	13	6	2	6	1236	2277.614	329,467
16. Kevin Cogan	25	14	4	1	13	1082	1912.752	331,962
17. John Andretti	23	5	4	0	0	514	935.016	123,760
18. Johnny Rutherford	23	15	8	0	0	1271	2155.214	347,775
19. Jeff MacPherson	21	15	6	0	0	1293	2100.256	352,357
20. Dick Simon	15	11	4	0	0	1020	1694.167	269,893
21. Randy Lewis	15	14	5	0	0	1174	2268.417	323,857
22. Scott Brayton	14	5	2	0	0	471	985.984	194,145
23. A.J. Foyt, Jr.	14	6	3	1	1	795	1349.464	163,572
24. Gary Bettenhausen	10	5	5	0	0	956	1746.000	195,238
25. Pancho Carter	9	8	4	2	49	807	1696.748	214,040
26. Chip Robinson	8	3	2	0	0	285	359.598	47,280
27. Raul Boesel	8	2	1	0	0	184	337.884	132,900
28. Scott Goodyear	7	7	4	0	0	472	976.802	119,479
29. Tony Bettenhausen	7	9	6	0	0	863	1685.314	192,877
30. Didier Theys	6	3	2	0	0	200	384.098	40,495
31. Dennis Firestone	6	2	1	0	0	229	251.780	35,250
32. Stan Fox	6	1	1	0	0	192	480.000	111,263
33. Jeff Wood	6	4	2	0	0	254	611.812	64,792
34. Ludwig Heimrath, Jr.	5	12	1	0	0	798	1453.157	284,786
35. Davy Jones	3	5	3	0	0	610	1045.332	158,127
36. Rick Miaskiewicz	1	4	1	0	0	217	475.270	53,340
37. Wally Dallenbach, Jr.	1	1	0	0	0	45	180.000	12,550
38. John Richards	0	4	2	0	0	222	454.854	46,710
39. Rocky Moran	0	1	1	0	0	86	143.620	22,300
40. Dale Coyne	0	8	2	0	0	243	542.364	146,301
41. Ed Pimm	0	2	0	0	0	287	628.500	107,087
42. Danny Ongais	0	2	0	0	0	194	384.544	19,038
43. Rich Vogler	0	1	0	0	0	109	272.500	98,263
44. Ian Ashley	0	1	0	0	0	56	99.904	3,275
45. Graham McRae	0	1	0	0	0	18	72.000	1,620
46. Gordon Johncock	0	1	0	0	0	76	190.000	94,913
47. Steve Chassey	0	1	0	0	0	68	170.000	97,913
48. Fulvio Ballabio	0	1	0	0	0	17	30.328	11,120
49. Dick Ferguson	0	1	0	0	0	19	38.000	9,536
50. George Snider	0	1	0	0	0	0	0.000	92,713
51. Mike Nish	0	0	0	0	0	0	0.000	14,000

1988 PPG INDY CAR WORLD SERIES
DRIVER PERFORMANCE CHART

DRIVER	POINTS	STARTS	RUN AT FIN	TIMES LED	LAPS LED	LAPS COMP (2067)	MILES COMP (3778.202)	PURSE
1. Danny Sullivan	182	15	11	24	517	1725	3133.932	$1,222,791
2. Al Unser, Jr.	149	15	10	14	339	1591	3099.712	1,004,256
3. Bobby Rahal	136	15	13	7	71	1925	3510.200	867,093
4. Rick Mears	129	15	11	15	475	1629	2907.673	1,414,472
5. Mario Andretti	126	15	7	17	240	1635	2870.037	712,091
6. Michael Andretti	119	15	11	3	3	1748	2987.423	887,187
7. Emerson Fittipaldi	105	15	7	12	231	1407	2556.632	942,636
8. Raul Boesel	89	15	9	2	6	1752	3098.099	597,052
9. Derek Daly	53	15	8	0	0	1398	2487.354	436,230
10. Teo Fabi	44	15	8	1	2	1217	1935.797	290,242
11. John Jones	44	14	9	0	0	1579	2818.193	359,525
12. Roberto Guerrero	40	12	5	0	0	1044	1859.366	345,706
13. Kevin Cogan	40	11	5	0	0	1037	1795.934	369,424
14. Arie Luyendyk	31	15	5	4	86	1202	1961.770	403,732
15. Didier Theys	29	8	5	0	0	547	1130.946	170,602
16. A.J. Foyt, Jr.	29	14	7	1	14	1259	2102.436	296,154
17. Tony Bettenhausen	25	12	5	0	0	1285	2138.890	268,667
18. Howdy Holmes	24	15	11	0	0	1643	2988.473	374,641
19. Al Unser	23	5	2	10	109	750	1627.001	320,020
20. Scott Atchison	17	13	8	0	0	1370	2427.651	235,531
21. Gordon Johncock	16	2	2	0	0	432	961.500	41,331
22. Phil Krueger	15	4	3	0	0	547	1246.600	168,954
23. Scott Brayton	12	12	4	1	11	1110	1768.366	293,125
24. Dick Simon	11	6	2	0	0	778	1446.000	212,944
25. Rocky Moran	9	10	4	0	0	740	1523.040	276,403
26. Bernard Jourdain	8	2	1	0	0	137	256.878	28,370
27. Jim Crawford	8	1	1	2	8	198	495.000	170,503
28. Ludwig Heimrath, Jr.	7	9	2	0	0	523	986.271	240,803
29. Randy Lewis	7	14	4	0	0	1123	2185.930	328,866
30. Billy Vukovich	6	4	3	0	0	688	1378.000	174,366
31. John Andretti	5	11	1	0	0	996	1713.114	268,068
32. Rich Vogler	2	3	1	0	0	508	1191.500	144,488
33. Dennis Vitolo	2	1	1	0	0	103	183.752	15,574
34. Dale Coyne	1	9	2	0	0	439	652.927	134,323
35. Ed Pimm	1	2	1	0	0	115	330.900	18,540
36. Ken Johnson	1	1	1	0	0	77	170.478	17,300
37. Jean-Pierre Frey	0	2	1	0	0	84	182.536	13,575
38. Scott Pruett	0	3	0	0	0	192	315.648	49,980
39. Fulvio Ballabio	0	3	1	0	0	105	295.110	23,795
40. Steve Bren	0	1	0	0	0	42	92.988	2,650
41. Dominic Dobson	0	4	0	0	0	230	536.754	138,143
42. Tero Palmroth	0	2	0	0	0	218	502.228	112,628
43. Johnny Rutherford	0	2	0	0	0	236	525.500	116,907
44. Darin Brassfield	0	2	0	0	0	61	139.534	14,770
45. Tom Sneva	0	2	0	0	0	125	266.000	114,805
46. Dick Ferguson	0	1	0	0	0	19	31.730	4,120
47. Steve Chassey	0	1	0	0	0	73	182.500	99,128
48. Stan Fox	0	1	0	0	0	2	5.000	113,703

1989 PPG INDY CAR WORLD SERIES
DRIVER PERFORMANCE CHART

DRIVER	POINTS	STARTS	RUN AT FIN	TIMES LED	LAPS LED	LAPS COMP (1973)	MILES COMP (3572.243)	PURSE
1. Emerson Fittipaldi	196	15	12	29	584	1958	3566.719	$2,166,078
2. Rick Mears	186	15	14	23	476	1952	3506.623	1,165,684
3. Michael Andretti	150	15	10	31	441	1931	3521.320	931,793
4. Teo Fabi	141	15	11	10	106	1646	2971.138	802,463
5. Al Unser, Jr.	136	15	11	8	148	1950	3508.652	1,247,571
6. Mario Andretti	110	15	10	9	77	1768	3276.119	759,364
7. Danny Sullivan	107	13	10	12	153	1482	2487.156	790,234
8. Scott Pruett	101	15	12	1	4	1791	3256.343	712,096
9. Bobby Rahal	88	15	9	4	67	1606	2793.929	687,424
10. Arie Luyendyk	75	15	11	0	0	1635	2937.080	541,445
11. Raul Boesel	68	15	11	1	1	1692	2962.113	662,821
12. Derek Daly	25	15	7	0	0	1389	2457.705	410,279
13. Pancho Carter	18	15	8	0	0	1252	2282.256	382,976
14. Kevin Cogan	18	14	6	0	0	980	1774.017	401,325
15. Scott Brayton	17	14	9	0	0	1684	3035.510	451,317
16. Al Unser	14	4	3	0	0	583	1335.440	196,786
17. John Jones	14	14	8	0	0	1494	2866.729	291,423
18. A.J. Foyt, Jr.	10	12	2	0	0	901	1648.132	347,579
19. Dominic Dobson	10	8	3	0	0	695	1353.758	223,456
20. Bernard Jourdain	10	14	5	0	0	1334	2424.084	343,770
21. Didier Theys	9	12	5	0	0	779	1569.744	304,541
22. Davy Jones	6	1	1	0	0	192	480.000	151,328
23. Roberto Guerrero	6	11	4	0	0	641	1454.204	196,119
24. Fabrizio Barbazza	6	8	2	0	0	361	804.371	140,060
25. Rich Vogler	5	2	1	0	0	194	484.000	170,896
26. Ludwig Heimrath, Jr.	4	7	2	0	0	536	1022.230	244,928
27. Johnny Rutherford	3	2	2	0	0	431	957.500	40,458
28. Tom Sneva	3	7	1	0	0	234	475.011	219,554
29. Guido Dacco	3	12	5	0	0	921	1487.618	137,003
30. James Weaver	2	3	1	0	0	129	247.420	37,564
31. Steve Saleen	1	7	5	0	0	473	1021.536	69,215
32. Jeff Wood	1	5	2	0	0	547	1151.505	100,300
33. John Andretti	1	6	2	0	0	369	868.654	175,832
34. Billy Vukovich, III	1	1	1	0	0	186	465.000	147,203
35. Randy Lewis	0	14	9	0	0	1214	2184.787	229,568
36. Jon Beekhuis	0	3	1	0	0	168	348.148	43,160
37. Scott Atchison	0	3	1	0	0	218	332.251	29,385
38. Rocky Moran	0	2	1	0	0	181	452.500	137,123
39. Geoff Brabham	0	1	0	0	0	89	171.058	19,240
40. Gordon Johncock	0	3	1	0	0	312	728.500	141,057
41. Jean Pierre Frey	0	2	1	0	0	136	218.058	16,820
42. Phil Krueger	0	1	0	0	0	189	378.000	14,039
43. Tero Palmroth	0	4	1	0	0	278	621.960	165,970
44. John Paul, Jr.	0	3	1	0	0	166	323.810	44,450
45. Scott Harrington	0	1	1	0	0	46	184.000	7,430
46. Fulvio Ballabio	0	2	1	0	0	135	270.340	21,770
47. Jim Crawford	0	1	0	0	0	135	337.500	119,403
48. Scott Goodyear	0	2	0	0	0	54	129.420	24,740
49. Mark Dismore	0	1	0	0	0	25	58.900	7,120
50. Tony Bettenhausen	0	1	0	0	0	13	32.500	16,231
51. Ken Johnson	0	1	0	0	0	6	13.284	9,620
52. Dale Coyne	0	1	0	0	0	4	10.000	16,094
53. Steve Chassey	0	2	0	0	0	15	19.821	28,813

1990 PPG INDY CAR WORLD SERIES
DRIVER PERFORMANCE CHART

DRIVER	POINTS	STARTS	RUN AT FIN	TIMES LED	LAPS LED	LAPS COMP (1973)	MILES COMP (3572.243)	PURSE
1. Al Unser Jr.	210	16	13	19	449	1853	3261.161	$1,936,833
2. Michael Andretti	181	16	11	15	512	1655	2916.121	1,303,526
3. Rick Mears	168	16	14	3	136	1979	3443.570	1,414,744
4. Bobby Rahal	153	16	14	11	222	1867	3320.704	1,462,458
5. Emerson Fittipaldi	144	16	13	10	412	1880	3259.634	1,513,176
6. Danny Sullivan	139	16	10	9	163	1495	2494.707	965,161
7. Mario Andretti	136	16	11	8	69	1515	2635.356	976,721
8. Arie Luyendyk	90	16	11	5	50	1584	2897.830	1,747,984
9. Eddie Cheever	80	16	11	0	0	1808	3182.450	869,720
10. John Andretti	51	16	8	0	0	1563	2722.013	456,594
11. A.J. Foyt Jr.	42	14	10	0	0	1403	2620.852	578,744
12. Raul Boesel	42	16	10	0	0	1504	2565.489	579,913
13. Scott Goodyear	36	16	12	0	0	1766	3069.881	429,724
14. Teo Fabi	33	16	8	2	27	1381	2336.946	614,335
15. Scott Brayton	28	16	10	0	0	1528	2667.624	592,442
16. Roberto Guerrero	24	15	5	0	0	1371	2400.354	471,375
17. Mike Groff	17	12	7	0	0	1029	1964.982	257.628
18. Didier Theys	15	12	7	0	0	956	1817.747	452,218
19. Dominic Dobson	12	11	5	0	0	734	1405.361	325,390
20. Pancho Carter	9	9	3	0	0	927	1508.000	323,967
21. Jon Beekhuis	7	9	2	0	0	559	1199.460	127,024
22. Jeff Wood	7	10	4	0	0	636	1133.123	117,269
23. Kevin Cogan	4	2	1	0	0	321	737.500	164,630
24. Tony Bettenhausen	4	11	6	0	0	773	1357.740	345,710
25. Dean Hall	4	15	9	0	0	1277	2350.415	444,735
26. Willy T. Ribbs	3	8	2	0	0	357	660.281	102,020
27. Wally Dallenbach Jr.	2	3	1	0	0	158	327.662	73,214
28. Randy Lewis	2	16	8	0	0	1231	2266.924	448,129
29. Guido Dacco	1	6	4	0	0	565	853.112	84,762
30. Buddy Lazier	1	6	2	0	0	435	694.298	178,031
31. Hiro Matsushita	1	10	4	0	0	586	1139.076	216,160
32. Michael Greenfield	1	7	0	0	0	405	615.639	69,350
33. Tero Palmroth	1	3	1	0	0	218	512.925	164,466
34. Billy Vukovich	0	2	1	0	0	312	675.000	148,787
35. Al Unser	0	1	1	0	0	186	465.000	141,387
36. Jim Crawford	0	2	1	0	0	229	503.500	140,272
37. John Paul Jr.	0	1	0	0	0	176	440.000	150,276
38. Joseph Sposato	0	1	1	0	0	76	168.264	4,250
39. Jeff Andretti	0	1	0	0	0	117	117.000	16,566
40. Ross Bentley	0	1	1	0	0	77	131.208	13,714
41. Geoff Brabham	0	1	1	0	0	161	402.500	131,688
42. Rocky Moran	0	1	0	0	0	88	220.000	124,580
43. Steve Bren	0	1	0	0	0	5	8.350	11,400
44. Tom Sneva	0	1	0	0	0	48	120.000	110,338
45. Gary Bettenhausen	0	1	0	0	0	39	97.500	109,464
46. Stan Fox	0	1	0	0	0	10	25.000	108,021
47. John Morton	0	0	0	0	0	0	0.000	10,212
48. Fulvio Ballabio	0	0	0	0	0	0	0.000	11,708
49. Salt Walther	0	0	0	0	0	0	0.000	0

1991 PPG INDY CAR WORLD SERIES
DRIVER PERFORMANCE CHART

DRIVER	POINTS	STARTS	RUN AT FIN	TIMES LED	LAPS LED	LAPS COMP (2107)	MILES COMP (3751.114)	PURSE
1. Michael Andretti	234	17	12	38	965	1911	3386.906	$2,461,734
2. Bobby Rahal	200	17	13	7	187	1865	3223.794	1,514,473
3. Al Unser Jr.	197	17	14	14	277	1866	3384.422	1,464,752
4. Rick Mears	144	17	11	14	230	1873	3355.484	2,369,865
5. Emerson Fittipaldi	140	17	11	11	120	1655	2848.510	1,201,473
6. Arie Luyendyk	134	17	12	10	207	1762	3229.234	1,142,194
7. Mario Andretti	132	17	12	7	102	1978	3500.813	1,037,217
8. John Andretti	105	17	13	2	5	1957	3385.939	904,855
9. Eddie Cheever	91	17	11	0	0	1791	3031.370	797,652
10. Scott Pruett	67	17	7	0	0	1490	2754.182	779,214
11. Danny Sullivan	56	17	8	1	2	1507	2722.708	753,156
12. Scott Brayton	52	17	12	1	12	1673	3059.762	722,234
13. Scott Goodyear	42	17	9	0	0	1247	2260.161	632,610
14. Tony Bettenhausen	27	17	13	0	0	1702	3178.894	632,757
15. Jeff Andretti	26	17	12	0	0	1685	2945.699	685,335
16. Mike Groff	22	13	6	0	0	1039	1931.566	507,422
17. Willy T. Ribbs	17	9	5	0	0	488	961.148	424,779
18. John Jones	10	10	4	0	0	817	1399.996	256,413
19. Ted Prappas	9	12	3	0	0	535	1044.099	240.253
20. Gordon Johncock	8	1	1	0	0	188	470.000	285,690
21. Paul Tracy	6	4	1	0	0	255	307.236	56,577
22. Buddy Lazier	6	9	3	0	0	274	605.996	283,525
23. Hiro Matsushita	6	17	14	0	0	1645	2810.316	535,596
24. Stan Fox	5	1	1	0	0	185	462.500	201,090
25. Didier Theys	4	9	3	0	0	402	775.907	217,365
26. Pancho Carter	3	3	0	0	0	430	758.000	193,229
27. Cornelis Euser	3	1	1	0	0	82	181.548	15,520
28. Franco Scapini	2	1	1	0	0	59	164.787	22,895
29. Randy Lewis	1	11	5	0	0	838	1610.150	433,138
30. Dean Hall	1	1	0	0	0	58	161.994	31,785
31. Gary Bettenhausen	1	1	0	0	0	89	222.500	177,890
32. Jeff Wood	0	8	3	0	0	365	827.937	191,070
33. A.J. Foyt Jr.	0	8	2	0	0	659	951.994	304,507
34. Dominic Dobson	0	1	1	0	0	164	410.000	159,190
35. Ross Bentley	0	1	1	0	0	90	150.930	32,220
36. Guido Dacco	0	4	2	0	0	278	472.642	47,200
37. Dennis Vitolo	0	4	0	0	0	228	303.399	38,952
38. Roberto Guerrero	0	5	2	0	0	234	515.332	188,708
39. Mark Dismore	0	3	1	0	0	231	292.556	62,446
40. Michael Greenfield	0	2	1	0	0	89	213.300	29,350
41. Al Unser	0	1	0	0	0	105	105.000	20,250
42. Bernard Jourdain	0	2	0	0	0	189	432.660	163,888
43. Phil Krueger	0	1	0	0	0	32	89.376	18,393
44. Geoff Brabham	0	1	0	0	0	109	272.500	136,491
45. Johnny Parsons Jr.	0	1	0	0	0	66	66.000	19,702
46. Dale Coyne	0	2	0	0	0	43	58.674	48,800
47. Nicola Marozzo	0	1	0	0	0	11	18.447	11,400
48. Tero Palmroth	0	1	0	0	0	77	192.500	131,990
49. John Paul Jr.	0	1	0	0	0	53	132.500	130,690
50. Jim Crawford	0	1	0	0	0	40	100.000	133,690
51. Kevin Cogan	0	1	0	0	0	24	60.000	127,391
52. Tony DeTommaso	0	0	0	0	0	0	0.000	0
53. Jon Beekhuis	0	0	0	0	0	0	0.000	10,952